The Plain Language of Love
and Loss

THE PLAIN LANGUAGE OF LOVE

AND LOSS

A QUAKER MEMOIR

Beth Taylor

University of Missouri Press
Columbia and London

For Barbara,
In honor of love
and art,
Beth

University of Missouri Press
Columbia and London
Copyright © 2009 by
The Curators of the University of Missouri
University of Missouri Press, Columbia, Missouri 65201
Printed and bound in the United States of America
All rights reserved
5 4 3 2 1   13 12 11 10 09

Library of Congress Cataloging-in-Publication Data

Taylor, Beth, 1953–
  The plain language of love and loss : a Quaker memoir / by Beth Taylor.
    p. cm.
  Summary: "A memoir of the author's Pennsylvania Quaker family and
the shadow cast on it by her brother's suicide at age fourteen during the
tumultuous Vietnam War era. Taylor grapples with understanding the
complexities of religious heritage, pacifism, and patriotism as she places
her family's story within the context of recent American history"—
Provided by publisher.
  ISBN 978-0-8262-1845-2 (alk. paper)
  1. Taylor, Beth, 1953- 2. Quakers—Biography. I. Title.
  BX7795.T29A3 2009
  289.6092—dc22
  [B]

                                                          2008049082

⊗™ This paper meets the requirements of the
American National Standard for Permanence of Paper
for Printed Library Materials, Z39.48, 1984.

Designer and Typesetter: Kristie Lee
Printer and binder: Thomson-Shore, Inc.
Typefaces: Minion, Bradley Hand, and Au Bauer Text Initials

For my mother and father,
for Daphne,
and for Geoff

CONTENTS

The Note   1

Hill of Vision   4

Into the Valley   32

Gentle Boy?   53

The Shadow of Death   60

Sister   69

Personas   80

Unpeaceable Kingdom   95

Family   108

Faith   124

ACKNOWLEDGMENTS

Many people lived through the early events of this story and I am grateful to all of them for their generosity and frankness, but mostly for their willingness to revisit a difficult time in all of our lives. Everything in this memoir is as true as I, or others, can remember it. All names are real, although I have used one person's chosen name.

I would like to thank the former and current members of Bryn Gweled Homesteads who shared their memories or who read early drafts: David Polster and his mother, Betty; Alice Maxfield and Nelson Camp; Susan and Bill Maxfield; Betsy Crofts; Alison Bass; Noel Hill.

I would like to thank my brother's school friends for their memories and honesty—Robert Stahl; Paul Seelig, Jr., and his father, the late Paul Seelig, Sr.; John Fesmire; John Stevenson; Rocky Tinari.

I would like to thank my cousins—Thompsons, Bronners, and Plaisteds, as well as friends Tony McQuail and his mother, Ginny, for their memories and insight.

I would like to thank my husband, Bill, and my boys, Pete, Sam, and Max—who did not ask to have a wife or mother who wrote publicly about them, but who accepted their roles in this story with grace.

I would like to thank my sister, Daphne, the one person in the world who has walked beside me every step of this story, for which I am grateful each day.

I am also grateful to the many readers whose insight and suggestions helped this manuscript evolve: Michael Ames, Tracy Breton,

Kris Dahl, Jody Lisberger, Andrew Blauner, Ladette Randolph, Kristen Rowley, Michael Bibby, Catherine Imbriglio, Jim Blight, and Janet Lang.

Finally, I am eternally grateful to Clair Willcox and his reader at the University of Missouri Press for deciding to take a chance on this story. And I thank the excellent staff of the UMP for shepherding this story where it needed to go.

The Plain
Language
of Love
AND LOSS

The Note

When I turned fifty, I stood at the kitchen counter looking out the window at our small backyard in Providence, Rhode Island, studying our one towering tree and old carriage house, and suddenly I saw my mother, alone at her kitchen table in Pennsylvania, looking out at her flower garden, the sloping lawn, the pear tree and woods beyond. It dawned on me that I was now as old as she had been when she lost her fourteen-year-old son to suicide. My mind didn't flash to my brother, Geoff. It saw only the three different faces of my own boys, each so full of life and purpose, and my breath caught. I could not fathom losing one of them. I saw my mother's face, the kindness of her smile, her attentive eyes, and I felt her spirit swirl through me even though she was now eight years gone. Sadness for her swept over me, into my bones, and I steadied myself against the hard countertop.

Soon after my mother died, I found a torn piece of white scrap paper, tucked into her college alumni magazine, lost among phone lists, newsletters, YWCA brochures, and letters from friends, in a box near her bed. I unfolded the paper. In her neat, clear handwriting, she had written "My son, Geoffrey Rowell Taylor, died." There was a space. Then, farther down the scrap of paper, in tighter script—as if her hand clenched—she wrote, "He was a good boy—" And the handwriting stopped again, for good.

She must have been in her early fifties when she wrote those words—notes for her college alumni news. When I found them, I sat on the

1

bed where she had died, and I tried to feel that moment as she stopped writing, thirty years earlier. What could she possibly say? In public. What words could sum up what that boy had been? List his accomplishments, his talents, his kindnesses, his triumphs, his wisdom, each time he was Geoff? What was the most essential word for him? He was a good boy. How true. How feeble a summary. How impossible to say what it felt to have known this boy, to have loved him, and now to have lost him. She knew all those college friends would want to know, would rally to her as soon as they knew, would write, even visit. But

Mom in kitchen writing at table.

Geoff with "bluebirds" stand.

she couldn't find the words. Any attempt immediately felt too loud, too empty, too harsh, too useless, so necessary, all at once. There was nothing she could say to explain what happened, because she didn't know, she didn't understand, it didn't make sense; the fact of his suicide was only a huge, yawning emptiness around her, inside her, sucking from her all the smart, capable, articulate words and energy that once filled her life with work and friends and love in ways that did make sense. She wanted to say something, to publicly say Geoff lived. But once she put pen to paper, stared at the first essential words, "he died," there was nothing more that mattered, nothing more to say. She was alone, deeply, profoundly isolated. Nothing, no words, no hug, no sympathy, would ever absolve her grief.

Before my mother died, she directed me through other boxes in her room—family heirlooms for my sister and me, useful goods for friends or donation, a few things for the trash. And then one day I opened boxes filled with newspaper articles and editorials—each one about the Vietnam War. The *New York Times*, the *Philadelphia Bulletin*, the *Saturday Review*, *Friends Journal*, *I.F. Stone's Weekly*—dating back to 1965, the year my brother died. "This is an archive, Mom," I said in wonder. She sat, exhausted, on her bed. "I thought I might write something," she mused. I had never known her to write anything for publication. But, I understood. I had begun to write about those years, and about Geoff, whose suicide had always seemed indirectly but inextricably tied to that war. Recently I had been interviewing old friends and discovering there were many ways to see what had happened in our family. My mother did not seem to mind. I had shown her an early draft of an essay. All she said was, "This writing that you're doing—is a good thing."

Hill of Vision

This is how they met. My mother was cleaning house, her hair tied up in a bandanna, when she greeted my father at the door as he came to pick up her roommate for a date. The next visit he took all three roommates to an alumni picnic at Haverford College, and decided right there he liked my mother's "milkmaid beauty" and her down-to-earth intelligence. They swapped tales of climbs up Mt. Washington, discovered they had probably been at the same USO dance in Petersham, Massachusetts, during the war, and then in Paris the same week, maybe at the Folies Bergère the same night. My father saw she listened well and seemed to enjoy his love for recalling stories, reciting poetry, and narrating family history. When he took my mother out on their first date, he stopped first to feed the chickens for his widowed mother at "Brooklawn" in Cheltenham, the old stone farmhouse that had been his boyhood home. He knocked on the henhouse door, asked his "ladies" if he might come in, and then he spoke French to them. Knowing she had grown up on a farm in Maine, he told my mother he was the closest to a farmer she would find in Philadelphia. But she was charmed by his urbane erudition, his energy, and his humor. That was the most important thing, she would often say—"He made me laugh."

Geoff was born ten months after they married. On a tiny cobblestoned alley in Philadelphia, not far from my father's law office, they squeezed up and down the spiral staircase of their three-story townhouse, one room on each floor, and dubbed it "The Casbah." When

Family
Christmas
Card.

MANY GOOD WISHES FOR GLADNESS AND CHEER –
A REAL MERRY CHRISTMAS
AND A HAPPY NEW YEAR.

Portrait of
Daphne, me,
and Geoff.

I came along, they decided it was time to find a place in the country. Through a former classmate of my father's they heard about a cooperative "intentional" community about twenty miles north of the city. Called Bryn Gweled—Welsh for "Hill of Vision"—it was founded in 1940 and carved out of two farms in Lower Bucks County. The founders wanted families to own the land together, share responsibility for common land, but build their own homes on a two- to three-acre "homestead." Beginning with twelve couples, they laid out their own plot boundaries on the 240 acres, dug the trenches so their electrical and phone lines could be underground, dug a communal pond and swimming pool, and debated their own by-laws to consensus. When a new couple wanted to join, they met each family on the Homesteads before they committed to become, and were accepted as, members.

As a charter member explained, it was supposed to be an "ideal community," free of prejudice and discrimination. They were artists, teachers, journalists, engineers, lawyers, and ministers. They were Quaker, Unitarian, Jewish, agnostic, and atheist. They were mostly white, but soon embraced the first black and Asian families to move to that suburban area. They described themselves with amusement as folks with "high ideals and low incomes"—although some of the founding couples had independent wealth that cushioned their abilities to risk living more by conscience than paycheck to paycheck. All chose to live by ideals less valued by mainstream America. Ed Ramburg left Europe before the Holocaust and helped found Bryn Gweled. In a community history he recalled, "We questioned the validity of authority—whether it was the authority of the government asking us to take part in war, or the authority of custom describing styles of living and spending of leisure time. Authority had not produced results which satisfied us. We hoped to develop a more brotherly and fulfilling way of life by applying our own judgment and experience, and such technical knowledge as we could gather."

By the time my parents joined in 1953, there were forty-three families. On one Saturday each month, men and women gathered for "work parties" to tend to the common areas—clearing underbrush near the skating pond, repairing road signs at the traffic circle, replacing lights in the community center, fixing the pump for the pool. For a while, the men collected the trash from each household on Saturday mornings, tossing bags into an old yellow pickup truck. Appropriately, when asked in second grade, "What does your father do?" my seven-year-old brother reported that his father was a trash collector. In the summer each family signed up for a week of cleaning-the-pool duty. While it was warm, everyone gathered on a Saturday for a picnic before the monthly meeting, where community business got debated and resolved with spirited discussion. We knew everyone by first name, and with some we shared a phone line. If a meeting was called or someone needed help with a crisis, we got a phone call through the "grapevine." We knew particular things that made us care about each neighbor, and we felt part of something larger than our own family.

For children, Bryn Gweled was a wonderful place to grow up. In the winter my brother, younger sister, and I met "the gang" at Morris's hill for a fast sled down toward the creek, or at the pond to skate. We gathered every summer evening with the kids on Woods Road or Hillside Road, and we built troll houses in the woods, or slid down the mud bank known as "The Big Moheaves," built dams on the creek, or played "Beckon" or baseball in the meadow till dark. When we wanted to know where a buddy was somewhere in BG, we'd give out a shrill, intense call—"Yey-ee-yeeet!" and if they were out there in the woods or on another road, they'd respond, the curt yodel leaping out of the

Geoff, with first model sailboat,
and me at swimming pool.

trees like an echo. On summer mornings, mothers offered courses in jazz dance, pottery, or weaving straw into baskets. In the steamy afternoons we oozed down to the Community Center to plunge gratefully into the cool, lifeguarded swimming pool. Swim down and back the first day, and you could go into the deep end. Swim ten laps without stopping, and you could come each afternoon without a parent—the cherished first step of independence. On hot summer evenings we joined buddies for a night swim or slept out under the stars on our lower lawn, lulled by the rhythmic whirr of the cicadas. Or, if it started to rain, we all crawled into the tent sheltered by the trees in our backyard, and listened to the tap-tapping of the drops as we told ghost stories and drew curly op art with flashlight beams on the dark green canvas.

My parents designed our house and loved its perch on a central hill that looked over the rolling former farmland. They positioned the picture window so the sun rose directly up its middle on December 21, and they created the fieldstone fireplace as the focus of the living room. Unlike their neighbors who chose the rectangle of the 1950s Frank Lloyd Wright houses, they remembered the snows of their youths and gave their roof a good pitch. Each Christmas they chose a live Christmas tree, and later, when the winter earth thawed, they planted it somewhere on the property, creating windbreaks that now tower over the house. To honor his Quaker heritage, my father planted ivy from William Penn's boyhood home in England, which my grandfather had first brought across the ocean to Brooklawn. From Maine, my mother brought blueberry bushes and a pine tree.

When the house was finished, my father took Geoff and me out to pick up stones from the raw earth before he planted soy to give protein to the dry, dusty dirt, then clover to feed the honeybees he kept in hives. As we grew older, he taught us how to smoke the bees before extracting the honeycomb, which we spun in a huge steel cylinder in our basement so the honey would fly out, coating the metal before it oozed through a trough into a jar. He showed our 4-H Club how to tap maple trees for sap, then heat it into syrup. One night he brought home fresh road kill and showed us how to skin and dry a small animal. On a Saturday each month, he took me into the musty smells of the Davis

Feed Mill to buy grain and oyster shells for my twenty-five chickens. My mother taught us how to make jelly from our dark blue grapes and applesauce from our red crabapples. We composted organic waste to go back into our garden, and hung a pail of fatty wastes after dinner in a tree so the raccoons didn't get it before the trash man came.

My father dubbed our family's three acres "Tobacco Road," which at first I thought referred to his pipe, nestled in one side of his mouth, emitting the sweet smell of walnut tobacco.

"Actually," he said, "there was a novel by that name, about folks in the South who had chickens running around, just like we do, and overgrown woods and gardens, just like we do."

On the hallway wall my mother posted a chore chart. Geoff did all the "boy" chores. He carried the trash bins out the fifty yards of our gravel driveway, mowed the half-acre of lumpy grass in the warmer months. In the autumn he helped my father insert the big storm windows and split wood for fires on the hearth. My sister and I were assigned indoor chores—dishes, washing and waxing the kitchen and bathroom floors, ironing, vacuuming, cooking, and setting the table. My tomboy spirit chafed at these girl duties, and I longed to mow the lawn or split some wood. In the meantime, we did often pull together as a family. When it rained too much and our furnace room flooded, we all set up the bucket brigade out the basement door—a process which, despite the wet clothes and dirt, always felt like fun for its humid sense of crisis averted and teamwork triumphant.

Our favorite visit in the warmer months was from the fish man. Geoff, Daphne, and I watched from the living-room window as he rumbled up the long, gravel driveway in his skinny refrigerator truck, turned a semi-circle in front of our flagstone porch, then eased himself out of the high front seat, dressed in rubber boots, fish-filthy pants, blue canvas jacket, and a black worker's cap jammed on his scruffy hair.

Right out of *Treasure Island*, I thought, imagining him on schooners in full sail, kicking over a bucket of slop in a rage, and hauling in the net full of fish for the day.

"Got shad today, Mrs. Taylor, or bluefish, or haddock," he said, his howdy-do smile revealing brown teeth.

We peered over the wooden slats holding in a huge pile of ice and saw google eyes staring out at us in frozen stoicism.

"Fresh from the dock," he would say, grinning at the three of us as we squinted up at him. "All the way from the docks of Philadelphia!"

My mother scrutinized the google-eyes a bit. "How long do you think the shad run might last?" she asked.

He shrugged. "A week? More?"

"We'd better get them while we can," she said. "Do you have any roe?"

I imagined the brown-black packets of fish eggs she would fry up with our eggs the next morning. I watched her appraise the fish and felt she was somehow back in her Maine element; she knew fish, and this guy's visit was always a treat for her in more ways than just dinner.

He flipped down the wood plank, pulled out three fish, flopped them down one at a time, took out a long, broad cleaver, and wumped the heads off. Each head he wrapped in newspaper and presented to one of us. He knew the routine: we promptly took our damp packages around the house to the front lawn, opened them like Christmas presents, and studied the silvery, shiny scales and eyes until my mother brought out the paring knives. Then we plunged delicately in, pulling back the skin, peering into the eye, probing to where the truncated backbone began.

"Yuk!" I'd spit in mock horror.

"Uuuum, good!" my brother would retort with relish.

Daphne stared at the colors as they changed from fresh glint to dull, dry gray.

One morning Geoff ran in from feeding our big collie dog to say a baby crow was flapping around out by the driveway.

"Can we help it?" he asked. "It probably fell out of its nest. Doesn't even know how to fly yet. Maybe its wing is broken."

My mother went to the window and studied the small, flapping black bird.

We had saved baby kittens and rabbits before when their mothers were hurt or killed, and once we nursed a sparrow that had crashed into our huge picture window. But a crow seemed a different challenge—among the bully species. In our Thorton Burgess books the crow was always the loud, obnoxious character; in Bryn Gweled they were overpopulating to the detriment of the bird neighborhood. But tolerance was the higher value.

"He probably doesn't have diseases yet," my mom said. "Get a box downstairs. Bring him on in."

Carefully, Geoff wrapped the bird in an old towel and placed it in the cardboard box. He fed it mush and milk with a dropper and slowly it calmed down. We found an old hamster cage in our basement to use as a home.

"I'll call him 'Poe the Crow,'" Geoff said, and he set the cage on the bureau next to our big, round kitchen table. Geoff's research on crows showed they were sociable and could even be taught to talk; by placing Poe next to us at our family meals, Geoff thought maybe he'd get the point and say a word. We all chatted with Poe, applauded when he felt good enough to eat on his own, and waited for him to finally move the hurt wing in a normal flap.

Geoff's friends were all waiting for the inaugural performance of the talking bird. But one afternoon, I came home late from school and Poe was gone.

"Geoff decided to let him go," Mom said.

"But what about making him talk?" I asked.

"Well," Mom said, "Geoff found out that to actually make a crow talk, you have to cut its tongue. I think he decided it was better for Poe to be free."

For weeks after, when we went out on the porch we would look toward the ridge across the road, where the crow families congregated in the grass. For awhile we could tell which was Poe; he was littler and took longer to take off when the big guys flew. Then, one day they all looked big and confident and we couldn't distinguish Poe anymore.

With the same openness they accepted the natural world, my parents spoke frankly about the facts of life. With my chickens, each of our cats, Geoff's dog, and Daphne's hamster and rabbits, we had plenty of reference points for knowing about sex and health and death. So one night, when the subject of pregnancy came up at the dinner table, my dad just cleared his throat and explained matter-of-factly that it was not so different for humans. That it happened when people were married. He described the anatomical logistics, and we stopped eating. The difference for humans, Dad went on to say, was that they needed to be in love, to be married. That was the important point. We weren't listening at this point because we had stopped short at hearing him say the word "penis." But we were flattered and proud that he could be so mature and straightforward with us. It sort of cleared the air and gave permission for further frank discussions down the road.

We did not sit down for dinner until my father was ready, after his nap or "grunt and groan" exercises to debrief him from his commute from his Philadelphia law practice. By the time he came to the kitchen Daphne and I had the table set and the cloth napkins furled in each of our initialed, silver napkin rings. My mother laid out a full, sumptuous meal each night in the tradition of her farm family—chicken or hamburger, ham, cow's tongue, chicken liver, fish, with beans or squash, beets, cauliflower, broccoli, and potato or rolls. We drank milk delivered in glass bottles to our door, and the occasional buttermilk—a treat for my father, which he gulped straight from the bottle to remind him of his childhood days when he'd skim the cream off the top of the milk bucket after milking his cow. We ate heartily and unfussily, never worrying about weight or diet. My father had the metabolism of an athlete well into his fifties. My brother was long and lean. Daphne and I became pudgy during puberty, but while she minded it, I tried hard to ignore it; I was out there playing baseball each summer night, sprinting faster than most boys in school races, and beating some of them in arm wrestling. My father hugged my mother's overweight body and chuckled that she was "pleasantly plump," that he liked a woman with "love handles." On weekend mornings when we were little, all three of us kids would crawl into her big bed and wrap our arms and legs around her generous, flanneled body, utterly content as we chatted and nudged each other with our feet.

Every night, after we had passed the serving plates, my father would say, "May we have silent grace, please?" And we each stopped scooping food, or unfolding our napkin, or fingering our silverware, and reached out to hold hands, then bowed our heads around the big, round oak table. We sat quietly, listening to the silence, and in a minute or so, after we felt calmed, my father squeezed my sister's hand, she squeezed my brother's hand, he squeezed mine, I squeezed my mother's, and she squeezed my father's, so the circle was complete. Then, as we started to eat, we each took turns reporting on our day, discussing upcoming projects, recounting funny comments overheard, or listening to family lore.

At the dinner table we learned many things, but in particular, that history is life, is how we judge ourselves, how we learn ways to live our own lives. We heard about our Quaker ancestors, the building of Philadelphia, and the ways of farming. Sometimes my father told us about his father, Francis Taylor, a lawyer and Quaker minister who had died before we were born. We knew Grandfather's law office was now my father's and we had visited on the occasional Saturday, looked out the window at the statue of "Billy Penn" atop Philadelphia's City Hall.

My father said his father was revered by all. Once, when Grandfather was about to give a speech, our Granna asked, Was he prepared? "Dear," he said, "I've been preparing for this my whole life." But he did have a sense of humor. Herbert Hoover invited Grandfather to preside over a Quaker worship in Washington. It was there, he loved to recall with a sly smile for his children, that as he recited Joel 2:28 in front of the president of the United States, he actually said, "Old men shall dream dreams, and young men shall see women—I mean, visions."

Grandfather founded the Cheltenham Bank, and during the Great Depression, to keep it from closing, he went to Washington to secure a loan. In a letter describing his character and his bank's worthiness during that difficult time, the investigating assessor wrote, "This man is incorruptible." My father would pause here, making sure the example sunk in. Incorruptible.

I understood it had not always been easy for my father to be his son. Grandfather was aggressive, fearless, my father said—like an Airedale dog, which was both good and bad. He made his family feel secure and protected, but he could be dictatorial, a tyrant. "Every once in awhile," my father said, "the pressure of his life would get to him and he would explode."

Our favorite stories were of my father's own life. Growing up on the last farm in Cheltenham, not far from the city, he liked guns, hunting, and trapping muskrats on Sandy Run Creek. He said he felt guilty because, despite being raised a pacifist, he was fascinated by the mournful stories of the Civil War, and he loved to play football because it was "civilized war." When World War II erupted, my father applied to be a conscientious objector. At first he was turned down because investigators found out he had liked hunting as a boy. But when my father appealed and Quaker elders spoke on his behalf, the board finally made him a C.O. and my father headed for two and a half years of alternative service. "If I wasn't going into the war, I was determined to prove my worth," he said. He scythed trails and dug water holes to fight forest fires near the Quabbin Reservoir in Massachusetts, then shoveled snow off roofs in the New Hampshire winter. He spent more than a year managing the violent ward of a Virginia mental hospital—where he got his shirt ripped off his back, a black eye, and a lump on his bald head from a guy wielding a shower pipe. Then he was sent west for a job as a smoke jumper fighting forest fires in Montana. Making those often terrifying leaps from planes into blazing mountainsides, my father said, "I finally met the physical challenge I'd been preparing for my whole life."

My mother told family stories cryptically, in between checking the stove and carrying food to the table. Often my father would prompt her, because she would not by nature think to talk so much about herself.

Our favorite was a story her parents had told her—of going to church in the harsh winter of 1916 when my mother was nine months old. In the old black sleigh, her mother, Frances, had wrapped my infant mother in white flannel and wool, then covered all three of them with a dark, furry buffalo hide. The horse was trotting along, across the cold, snowy fields of their farm, not far from the ocean in Maine, when something happened—a tree branch snapped, a bird flew up. The horse took off, terrified. Her father, Leon, held tight to the reins, but Frances knew about runaways—they always swerve or crash. So she pulled the flannel up over my mother's face and she looked ahead for drifts that could mean softer snow. Finally, she braced her legs and tossed my infant mother, a perfect soft pitch, into the air as she prayed. Dear God. Dear God. And then she jumped too, into the air, hitting hard against the cold, icy snow. She found my mother crying, but OK. Then everything got quiet, even my mother, as Frances waited

Geoff and me
with Mom and
Grandparents
(Plaisteds).

for Leon and the sleigh to come swishing back, his hands purple-red under his gloves from gripping the reins so hard. Thankful.

Frances Plaisted raised her children to be faithful Baptists, and she "ruled the roost," my mother said, a complement to her kind, quiet husband who avoided confrontations and was happiest puttering at his workbench. When snow buried the farmhouse and the men were out in the barn helping the animals, it was Frances—5'3", barely seeing over the snowdrifts—who dug the path for my mother and her younger brothers to catch the bus. When my mother neared high school, they moved a few miles inland, closer to town, and Leon left farming behind to become an electrical engineer, helping to bring electricity for the first time to the mills around Sanford.

Besides being the resourceful daughter—cooking, cleaning, sewing—my mother helped care for her brothers, organized the cousins at family gatherings, earned good grades, performed in plays at school, and won awards as a Girl Scout. In high school she worked weekends and summers at Woolworth's so she could pay her way through college, maybe even go to a Seven Sisters college as her English teacher suggested. But it was 1933, and the bank closed and she lost all her savings. Her aunt helped pay her way to Keene State Teacher's College in New Hampshire, and then in her first teaching job, my mother saved enough money to pay back the loan. When World War II hit, her brothers joined the Navy and Army Air Force. My mother was teaching in New Hampshire, but soon, wanting to be a community organizer, she moved on to administrative positions with the Girl Scouts and the YWCA in New York City.

She said her most dramatic experience before we came along was just after the war, when she led a trip of youth hostelers bicycling through Europe. Stunned by the devastation in London and Paris, they sold their bikes so they could buy materials to repair a bombed-out hostel. Then they headed for an International Youth Conference in Norway where they tried to share the lessons of their particular war. She had always been interested in the varieties of religious experience, and in meditative ways of life that encouraged unity rather than exclusion or divisiveness. Her trip to postwar Europe cemented a deep commitment to pacifism, she said. When she returned to the States, she was hired to organize work camps for the American Friends Service Committee in Philadelphia. It was there in 1950 she met my father as he dated her roommate, and her inclination toward Quakerism found intrigue in his thoroughly Quaker credentials.

Often at dinner, in a sentimental or philosophical mood, my father would quote Shakespeare, or poets like Keats or Rupert Brooke—"If I should die, think only this of me / That there's some corner of a foreign field / That is forever England." I would listen to his dramatic voice, hear the lyricism of the words, and conjure vivid images in my mind. Appreciating older forms of language was as important as knowing our history. That's why, to underscore our sense of Quakerism, my parents chose to do as my father's family had done for generations: they raised us to use the plain language—thee, thy, thine—among family and with Quaker elders of the Philadelphia Yearly Meeting. "Will thee have some more ham?" "Get thy coat, please." "Is that book thine?" To Geoff, Daphne, and me, speaking the plain language among ourselves was like breathing, a way of speaking we didn't ever think about until occasionally someone would hear us talking at school and startle us by asking about it. To acquaintances, if at first it sounded odd, it quickly sounded charming, even comforting. For my mother, who learned it as my father's wife but who practiced it every day, thees and thys sounded natural; but when she occasionally got frustrated with us, she would lapse into "YOU!" and we would be chastened. "You" meant disaffection, and it hurt.

At the dinner table my father intertwined language lessons with school lessons. "OK precious bairns," he'd say. "By the way, that's Scottish for barn child, and it sounds like bar, the German word for bear, so I like it because you are my little bears, and you have one German family by marriage in your lineage, so it's still a good word for us." Then, back to the lesson: "If a farmer had three pigs and he went to market to buy some more pigs, but he only had ten dollars and each pig cost three dollars, how many could he buy and how much would he have left over to buy some grain?" Geoff and I would race to figure out these word problems, intrigued by the necessary visualization even as our hearts pounded, scared we would err. But we usually figured them out. Daphne had a harder time with such on-the-spot challenges. My father would push her, gently, explaining the problem once again until she got it. If she became flustered, he usually stopped and changed the subject. But there came a time when I realized he was frustrated with her seeming disinterest in these table games, and he started to goad her: "What's the matter? Thee can do this! Just like Geoff and Bethy at thy age! It's not going to get any easier, honey. Thee just try again, right now—no, don't pout, let's go . . . One more time . . ." I remember the night Daphne finally burst into tears, and I felt for the first time some fear and hatred of my father for bullying her. "Clearly," I thought, "All she wanted to do was eat dinner, so lay off!" At the table that night, we ate for awhile in silence. Then my father reached over, patted her hand, and brought up something new to talk about.

My own impudence sometimes burst forth in these otherwise pleasant family dinners. I don't remember the specifics, but I do remember that I awoke on my seventh birthday promising to behave better and to not talk back or hurt anybody's feelings. I was assertive, quick to get the last word, often using humor and my "dramatic flair" to deflect tension or discomfort. A photograph of me as a kid shows a group of us outside Southampton Friends Meeting, with everyone smiling, but me sticking my tongue out. That rebellion made me bold so that instinctively I was skeptical of authority, even as I feared it and obeyed.

When I was ten, I remember shaking my head at the dinner table over something my father had said, and blurting sarcastically, "Yeah, right!" There was a sudden pause. And then he reared up, his face red, his fist clutching his white napkin as he stabbed the air toward the stairs near him and said with cold fury, "GO to thy room, NOW!" I rose clumsily from my seat across from him, surprised by his rage, and backed away into the living room behind me, hoping to get to the stairs by going around the long way so as to avoid him. But as I sprinted toward the stairs, he was right there at the bottom step, and as I took a hurtling leap up the steps, his hand found my bottom with a resounding thwack. I spent a dinnerless night in my room fuming at his tyranny, and then felt grateful the next morning when I entered the breakfast-busy kitchen, with my mother once again at the stove, now making eggs and toast, my father now behind the paper with his coffee, and both of them greeted me with their usual "Good morning, Bethy!" Life would go on.

My mother's take on life meant always finding ways to placate, distract, and create. While my father was at work, she allowed us to take over the living room and build forts or large houseboats for our dolls, using wood blocks as bricks. Or we spread a board game over the rug for hours. When the house was new, before we painted our bedroom walls, she let us draw all over them—multicolored collages of figures, doodles, and words. Sketch pads, cloth and thread, building tools, glues, paints, charcoal, Craypas, magic markers, pencils were always ready. For a treat, she drove us to the Hobby Shop or Ollard's Stationery store. We liked manufactured, paint-by-number landscapes as well as the plastic bird models we could fit together and paint. But making presents, sewing one's own clothes, creating one's toys, were all considered more valuable than anything store-bought.

During summer vacations, Geoff would sit quietly beside my mother on a cottage porch in Maine or on the white sand of New Jersey, each of them holding an easel on their lap, each of them looking out, studying, then looking down, moving their hands quickly, then slowly, sometimes erasing, sometimes murmuring to the other as they sketched the landscapes—of Maine pines, coves, and rocks, of New Jersey waves, dunes, and sailboats. Daphne soon joined them with a sketchbook, while I, not drawn to the patience and mess of charcoals or watercolors, headed off with my Instamatic camera, clean and quick in its capture of the interesting shapes and dramas of the world.

Each time I went down to the basement—to carry the laundry out to the clothesline, to iron some shirts, to find a rake—I'd look toward the workbench to see Geoff's newest project. One winter a landscape for his Lionel train set sprouted on a huge plywood table—plaster hills, covered with green grass, twig trees, crushed gravel roads, and electricity wired to streetlights and a train station. In the summer, he built model sailboats—balsa wood hulls, lead keels, dowel masts, the boom tied to the tiller wire for self-sufficiency on the water, and toothpicks stitched into the sails to stiffen the cloth against the wind on the pond at the bottom of our hill.

One summer, Geoff asked my mother to buy him a huge piece of muslin, and he cut and sewed a real sail, then raised it on a mast he made for an old canvas kayak. Dad and I helped him load it on top of the station wagon and drive it first to the Churchville Reservoir and then down to the New Jersey shore—where he sailed it with surprising grace as I stood on the sandy bank, photographing his triumph. The next winter he nailed skate blades on a ten-foot-long, triangular wood frame, put the mast and sail on top, and raced his "ice boat" on the pond.

For weeks before Christmas when Daphne was nine, Geoff shooed us from the basement during the early winter snows and hung bed-sheets so we couldn't see his workbench if we came down to do the laundry. He built a three-story Swiss chalet for her small, dimpled trolls—with a tree-bark roof, round windows with screens, electric lights and "fire" in the fireplace, rocking chair, beds and table, and stairs up to the second floor. He asked our neighbor Sarah to paint a mini-portrait of Grandma Troll for the wall, and to sew a miniature braided rug, tiny stuffed mattresses, sheets, and quilts for the beds.

The next summer Geoff lashed together a campsite in our woods—table and benches made of branches between trees.

I begged him to teach me. "All I do at Girl Scouts is drip tea bags on the margins of the Beatitudes to make them look old!"

He smiled. "I have to learn this for the Scout jamboree."

"So?"

"We have to compete—time-wise. I have to be fast."

"Yeah, so?"

"So the more I do this in different ways all by myself, the faster, more confident I get."

I rolled my eyes. "So watch, at least," he said, grasping the end of a long branch he had cut. "And help me by holding up the other end back there so this end is perpendicular to the trunk."

"Then I can't see what thee's doing."

"Yeah, well . . . Call Daph and make her hold up that end. Then I'll show thee."

Daphne was busy helping Mom make Jell-O, the glass bowl waiting on the big round table in the kitchen. She stood on the step stool to be high enough to stir when Mom brought over the boiling water from the stove. Daph's light brown pixie haircut framed her face as she bent over, studying the green granules against the clear glass. "Uh-uh," she shook her head when I told her we needed her down at the campsite. She knew from experience we would give her the least attractive job, the same way we would leave her lagging behind in a hike—to the sledding hill, to the skating pond, to each neighbor as we sold tomatoes from our wheelbarrow. "Mom and I are busy."

So in the end, I watched Geoff as best I could, his lean body in cut-off jeans and a dirty white T-shirt, his strong hands winding and lashing the bristly rope, to the left, down, under, up, in patterns that made sense, it seemed. And I sort of got it. At Girl Scout camp that summer, as my unit of girls stood in a clearing for a rope-lashing session, I boasted to my counselor I knew all about lashing campsite furnishings. She looked at me doubtfully. I hoped my fellow scouts were looking at me with admiration.

"OK," my counselor said, watching my face. "What's the first rule of lashing in the woods?"

Rule? I thought. Rule? Geoff said nothing of "rules." He just did it and I watched, so give me some rope and I'll show you. I stared at the counselor, my cheeks flushed with embarrassment.

She smirked. "Best not to open one's mouth unless one knows what one is talking about. It could be dangerous in the woods."

My feet seeped sweat into my new sneakers, and I knew the girls, all neatly decked out in short green shorts, white blouses, and lanyard ties, were glancing at me, raising eyebrows at each other, as the counselor's wolflike grin howled in my brain: hoo hoo hee hee, git ya there smarty pants! Grrrrrr. This was the difference between Geoff and me, I thought. He actually knows how to do it—anything. I know ABOUT it, sort of, by watching—which is never the same as doing.

I found my niche in photography. I liked its realism and was fascinated by the mechanics of cameras and the chemistry of the darkroom. I supported my expensive habit with egg money. My father had dubbed me "Vice President, in charge of Sales" of our twenty-five chickens, and showed me how to keep the account books on the cost of raising them, then the balancing income they brought in as I sold their eggs. My neighbor Sue, an art student, took me into Philadelphia to help me find my first good camera. Then Geoff helped me build a darkroom in the basement bathroom, designing a table that fit over the toilet and around the sink so I could enlarge prints in the damp dark. Soon I was photographing Friends' weddings, taking newspaper and passport portraits, and competing in 4-H Club exhibits—trying to capture history as it happened.

Every Sunday our family drove quietly to Quaker Meeting—Daphne and I dressed neatly in hand-me-down skirts and blouses, Geoff in khakis and dress shirt. I loved the white-walled Quaker Meeting room, filled with simple wooden benches; families, individuals, and couples sitting in silence, pursuing some thought or watching the meditative faces of the Elders on the Facing Bench; learning as we grew older to wade past our superficial concerns to that deeper place of uncluttered peace. In the summer that journey was punctuated by birdcalls outside the open windows, and by the colorful sweetness of wild and garden flowers filling the vase up front. The place I was able to enter in Meeting—silent and calm—felt like a kind of anchor, and offered a way of knowing that went deeper than books or teachers.

As kids, after twenty minutes of worship with the grown-ups, we left for First Day School where we put words and understanding to our silence. We sang hymns—"For the Beauty of the Earth," "This Is My Father's World," or folk songs—"'Tis a Gift to Be Simple, 'Tis a Gift to Be Free." Older kids like Geoff took turns reading aloud a passage from the Bible. In smaller classes, we learned our Quaker history—Mary Dyer hung on Boston Common for preaching Quakerism after the

Puritans banished her "cursed sect of heretics"; Elizabeth Fry comforting the imprisoned in eighteenth-century England; John Woolman writing against slavery in eighteenth-century Pennsylvania.

My favorite story was of William Penn. When called before the king in the 1670s, he stood there, refusing to remove his broad black hat because Quakers believed all must cover themselves equally before God. Then he addressed the king as "thee" instead of the more respectful "you" because, again, all were equal in the eyes of God. The king smiled at William's subversion. "Well then William Penn, if thee doesn't mind, I will keep my hat on too," and he tapped his regal cap in wry acknowledgment.

On a spring trip with some of our Quaker cousins, we visited Penn's Manor on the banks of the Delaware River. Red brick and solid, it looked more English and formal than the narrow white farmhouses of Pennsylvania architecture. A docent greeted us, dressed in plain, Quaker garb—white apron over long gray dress, no buttons, a white cap snugly tied under her chin. She told us the story of Penn petitioning King Charles II for land to start a Friends colony, his "Holy Experiment." She showed us the Quaker painting by Benjamin West, of Penn standing under a huge elm tree on the Delaware River, his arms spread open as two Quaker men kneel and offer a bolt of cloth to the chief of the Delaware Indians. And then *The Peaceable Kingdom* by Edward Hicks, inspired by Isaiah: "The wolf shall dwell with the lamb, and the leopard shall lie down with the kid . . . They shall not hurt nor destroy in all my holy mountain." In the muted greens and browns of the painting animals and children rest side by side, while in the background Quaker men, dressed in broad black hats and simple jackets, hold the peace treaty signed with the Indians by William Penn.

Geoff, Daphne, and I absorbed these stories and images so they became touchstones, a foundation of history beneath my father's and mother's family stories. The key images of negotiation, humility, compassion, and simplicity seeped into us, inspiring if also a bit daunting. I wondered if William Penn had been fearless like my grandfather, or if he sometimes lost his temper like my father.

My father's school reunions gave us a glimpse into how he, with his robust energy, had dealt with Quaker strictures when he was young. Each May we followed him—nattily dressed in his blue-striped, seer-

Dad at Alumni Day.

sucker suit, bow tie, and straw boater atop his bald head—to the class gatherings at Westtown School and Haverford College, each founded by Quakers. We played with the kids of classmates my father had known, in some cases since second grade. Now professors, homemakers, lawyers, businessmen, doctors, teachers, and artists, these friends, mostly Quaker, were his extended family beyond our blood relatives. They enjoyed an easy camaraderie born of shared values—many of the men had been conscientious objectors performing alternative service in World War II—and the loyalty of so many years spent crossing paths, caring about each others' families, sharing each others' success, struggles, and losses.

At Westtown, we kids ran in packs over green lawns and through cool hallways, where we stopped to find, among the many black-and-white photographs of stiff-looking, plain-dressed people, the portraits of a parent or grandparent, or in some cases both parents and grandparents. Sometimes Geoff, Daphne, and I overheard the stories classmates told about our father, how he was always being disciplined at Westtown—for talking when he shouldn't, for coming to dinner late, for being at the lake with a girl after hours, for setting off an alarm clock in silent meeting for worship. At Haverford we heard how he almost outran the seniors in the freshmen hazing ritual of being chased, caught, and paddled; how he and his six-foot-tall college roommate dressed up as nuns to sneak into a Bryn Mawr "no men allowed" play, but were caught when someone noticed their big feet sticking out beneath their habits; how he was benched in a baseball game because he got back too late from a trip to see a girl; and how he had set records as an All-American soccer player. That last was of particular interest to Geoff, as he was already a standout in soccer at age twelve, and knew that Haverford was the college my father hoped, even assumed, he would attend.

In summers cousins and friends came out to Tobacco Road in Bryn Gweled, and we'd set up tables on the terrace, prepare baked chicken or sliced cold ham, beans, lettuce, corn, and tomatoes from the garden, and desserts made from our blueberries, blackberries, or rhubarb. I would tire of the constant kitchen preparations, but loved the camaraderie and then the pick-up baseball games or firefly chases among the kids as the darkness settled in, the grown-ups quietly chatting on the terrace.

A favorite visit was from our Thompson cousins, the children of my father's sister Marge. Although they had moved to Pittsburgh and then Missouri, they kept in frequent contact and often stopped by on trips back east to see old friends, family, and schools. Humor seemed to lighten the Quaker legacy in their family, and their son Rick felt like an older brother to us—teasing, cheerful, and knowing. Like my brother he was an only son with two sisters, so he and Geoff understood something in each other. They took off on bird walks—no girls allowed. Or they disappeared for hours at a time to our campsite, lashing and whittling, enjoying the pleasure of building something from nothing but trees, an axe, rope, and a shovel.

I loved Rick for his goofy jokes and worn red baseball cap with the curly white "P." We called him "Maz" for his passionate love of the Pittsburgh Pirates and their star second baseman, Bill Mazeroski. The summer of 1961 he entertained us as we sat, crammed into the sunny way-back of the Pontiac station wagon, and headed off to the beach in New Jersey, the hot air battering us through the open car windows.

"A home run!" Maz yelled, his voice cracking, grinning as he told the story one more time. "The END of the ninth inning! The END of the FINAL game! He WON the series! And it was the YANKEES!"

Soon Rick and Geoff were swapping sick jokes from Mad Magazine, pulling their ears out like Alfred E. Newman. They came to a particularly gruesome end to a "Spy vs. Spy" joke. Daphne and I grimaced at each other. "That's disgusting!" we yelled over the loud rush of hot air. And the boys cackled like we just didn't get it.

Each July, for a week or two, we stayed in a rickety old fisherman's shack on the wide, white sands of Shipbottom, on Long Beach Island. For my mother, with the help of a teenager from Bryn Gweled to watch out for us, it was a chance to relax. But first, packing the car was a paramilitary operation. Suitcases, food boxes, towels, beach umbrella, beach chairs, cleaning products, inner tubes, blankets—Geoff and I hoisted cumbersome packages to the station wagon roof so Dad could strap everything down under the old green canvas. Or we shoved and crushed till my mother's last-minute bags fit in the way-back, around the pillows where we kids would sit.

One year I ran into the kitchen to get one more bag just as my father yelled, "Dottie goddammit, come-on!" and I found my mother, bowed over the sink, finishing the last of the breakfast dishes, sweat pouring down her face and arms. She wiped a drop off her nose.

"Let's go, Mom," I said, scared by my father's impatience.

She turned to me, her eyes red with furious tears. "I'll—be—right—there," she said between gritted teeth.

In that moment I suddenly understood how hard she worked for us, and how unappreciated she felt. I promised myself if my father dared to yell at her again I would glare at him.

By the time we piled into the car, flew down the highway with the windows open to the hot, noisy air, and made it across the causeway to the coolness of the shore, all anger was forgotten, or at least moved behind us. JJ, the babysitter, took over and my parents went out to dinner, or had the cottage to themselves while we kids took off for miniature golf.

The three of us, and sometimes cousins, slept in sagging iron cots covered in thin, white coverlets, eye-level to windows under the roof that looked out over the dunes toward the broad expanse of the gray-green Atlantic. It was a week of squinting in the brilliant sun, scrambling toward the bell of the popsicle man, deliberating over penny candy at Ackers, braving forceful waves, digging for sand crabs, walking along the beach to the jetty, then leaping from one huge, gray chunk of granite to another till we reached the moment of spray exploding up into our thrilled, scrunched faces. As I walked with my mother beside the ocean, collecting shells and sea glass, she explained the ways of starfish and sand dollars and asked me about the book I was reading or how a friend was doing these days. But mostly we walked quietly, looked away from the crowds on the beach and out toward the wide expanse of sea, enjoying a solace without words.

In August we packed again into the station wagon and drove up to Maine, arriving at my mother's parents' house late in the afternoon. The five of us would pile out of the station wagon, stiff and cranky, and Geoff would make a beeline for the garage, where Grampa was always working at his workbench, oiling a part for his ancient car, "The Green Hornet." Gramps would chuckle in his hard-to-breathe way as he showed Geoff the metal part in his blackened hands. Prob-

At the beach.

ably not much got said between them in the next two hours as they worked side by side. The rest of us headed in to the musty coolness of the mudroom behind Grammy's neat kitchen, and to Grammy, blind from glaucoma, waiting to wrap her arms around each one of us.

The next day we would head for the family camping area my mother's brother Bob had carved out of the old Plaisted farmland not far from Sanford. We pitched our tent, set up the Coleman stove and clotheslines between trees, then settled in to life in the woods. On muggy afternoons, we swam in the muddy pond dug from the brook, which once graced a meadow of hay that my great-grandfather Plaisted harvested. Or we headed for the ocean at Ogunquit or Kennebunk, where we swam and checked in with our older Plaisted cousins as they worked summer jobs near the boardwalk. As evening fell we gathered as families and promenaded around the campsites to light the candles under hurricane glass at the entrance to each outhouse. Other campers fell in to join us, and we followed my Aunt Polly as she squeezed her accordion and led us down the dirt paths, between the dark trees now looming in shadow, singing as we strolled—"We are marching to Pre-toria, Pre-toria, Pre-toria. We are marching to Pre-toria, Pretorii-a-a-I-ay!"

Other cousins—cousins we thought of as living in the "real" Maine because they lived in trailers and ran flea market stalls or worked as bridge builders, waitresses, and mechanics—came for picnics and evening "ghost walks" where the bigger boys scared the younger girls with haunting hoots and disembodied wails from the dark night woods. One night they declared it was time for a "snipe hunt," our prey a mythical, small, hard-to-define creature that only came out after sundown. Geoff joined the older boys as they loped off into the gloom of the trees beyond the clearing.

"You girls come in ten minutes!" he called back to us.

As we waited, Dottie, my age and named for my mother, teased me for our city ways. "Whatchamean ya don't know how t' drive a cah yit?"

"Well, there are laws, you know," I said, envious at the freedom I suddenly realized she had on a rural road.

I pulled out my penknife and we started carving our initials into a tree, using a flashlight to see.

"Bitch bahk is the best," Dottie said.

"This is bitch bahk? You are so rude!" I said, grinning. "Just TRY to say those Rs, Dorothy: birrrrrch barrrrrrk!"

I felt kindred; because we had learned language from my mother's Maine accent before we entered school in Pennsylvania, for our early years all three of us dropped and added Rs in odd places: the neighbor girl's name was Linder; we needed a drink of waa-dah. Going to Maine was coming home in a way.

When he was thirteen, Geoff spent a blissful month helping to run the camping area. He and the Plaisted cousins constructed a huge tepee, built picnic tables, chopped campfire wood, and responded to campers' needs. He seemed particularly charmed by our cousin Becky, who was about his age and whose humor, athleticism, and skills at cooking or wood chopping defined for him the ideal girl. But somehow the only way he knew to show his admiration was to sneak up one day and lock her in the outhouse, leading to a rare outburst of fury in her, yelling and pounding on the wood-slatted door until the incident became part of family lore.

In the autumn, as the air cooled, our lives settled back to the orderliness of school schedules. Pumpkin and squash vines sprawled through gardens and Bryn Gweled celebrated the community with its Fall Festival. Grown-ups and kids joined in a rag-tag soccer game on the field of the Community Center. Bigger kids set up booths for the younger kids. Geoff designed and built a paint-spinning machine, sticking a plastic bucket onto a miniature rotation engine. Using my father's shirt cardboards for canvases and squirt bottles filled with paints, he helped the rest of us create our first op art. Another autumn, he drew a poster reporting the migration patterns of bluebirds and proposing ways to lure them to BG. I studied the graphs and exposition, admired his precise illustration of a bluebird, inspired by an Audubon drawing. Soon after, on a crisp Sunday afternoon, my father and Geoff led us up Hawk Mountain, scrambling toward a bluff on the ridge so we could look out over the red, yellow leaves of the Pennsylvania valley, searching for the legendary bald eagle.

On Thanksgiving Day, we visited my father's sister Anne and family on the Haverford campus, where her husband, Ed Bronner, curated the Quaker Collection at the college. In their home, we walked into the calm quiet of a library, or of life as we assumed it had been lived in my father's and Anne's youth—full of books, proprieties, and contemplative silence. We played games like "Author"—with cards showing the stern faces of Louisa May Alcott, Nathaniel Hawthorne, Edgar Allan Poe, or Henry Wadsworth Longfellow. A bookworm already, I felt right at home: I lived in the books I loved—*Little Women, Penrod and Sam, The Five Little Peppers.* But in this home, I was also a bit wary. All the weight, sobriety, and seriousness of our Quaker heritage seemed to govern their family dynamics. We were careful of our behavior and respectful in all conversations, even with the four girls. But we enjoyed the ritual of the formality like a game strategy to be gleaned and mastered, kind of like school.

As the days shortened and snow flurries dusted Tobacco Road, Geoff carried in the split wood from the porch and built the "log cabin" fire in our fireplace. In the evening we often sat near the warmth of the flames and listened to my father read. *The Story of Kennett,* about the highwayman Sandy Flash, or *Monarch the Big Bear,* the huge, old

Geoff with best friend David and op art paint machine.

legend who wouldn't die, no matter how many bullets the bully hunters pumped into him. During those nights Geoff sat by the fire on a stool he had built and whittled sticks for a model stockade for his miniature cowboys and Indians, or he carved chunks of soap into a Nativity scene for Christmas. Daphne and I knitted or crocheted, and Mom mended our socks. Like our Bronner cousins, we were a family out of the nineteenth century more than the mid–twentieth century. We had no TV—except a rental for Olympics and elections. I sometimes envied kids at school who talked about TV shows and rock bands I didn't know. And I felt hurt and embarrassed when a boy called me "Trailblazer" for my sturdy brown shoes, or another asked if we had a still out there in our woods. But on those nights around the hearth, listening to my father's deep, dramatic voice, I didn't feel odd or out of step; I only felt content, and challenged, and loved.

When the deep snows came, we wrapped up in scarves and mittens knitted by my father's mother. I broke the ice on the chickens' trough each morning, then tried hard to keep up with Geoff as he shoveled the driveway, built an igloo in a snowdrift, or strapped on our parents' long wooden skis for a slide down the meadow. One winter Geoff organized an ice hockey team on our community pond.

"Can I come?" I asked.

"These are fast guys. They know what they're doing." Geoff worked on the laces of his ice hockey skates.

"So do I," I bluffed. "I'm just as fast. Or, I'll play goalie. How's that?"

"Goalies get hurt. Dad and Mom would never let thee." He finished threading the laces and then pulled up his wool socks, tucking his blue jeans into them neatly.

"I'll wrap padding around my legs," I said, knowing I had offered an appealing option by relegating myself to goalie status.

"Not today. But I'll ask around. Maybe somebody has some goalie stuff."

"Well, I'm coming down anyway. Allie too. She's just as good as me."

"Yeah, I guess."

I grabbed my skates.

Down at the pond, buffeted by wind, and hunkered around the logs set out as benches, the other guys said nothing as Allie and I followed

Geoff onto the ice. I knew they admired him too much to challenge his decision even though we were the only girls who wanted to play. A few days later, someone found some goalie pads, someone else donated a baseball catcher's vest and glove, my father bought a goalie mask, and I was set to take the flip shots from Geoff's friends—and Allie too.

The Saturday before Christmas, our family joined dozens of Bryn Gweleders in the snowy woods behind a neighbor's house to sing carols around a shaggy old pine—lit up with blue, red, and green bulbs, rising high above us against the cold, dark night. We kids ran in and out of the glass-walled house, refilling our cups of hot cider, warming our feet on the heated cement floor. Then, on Sunday, we joined other Quaker families in the small Southampton Meeting House for an evening candlelight service. Warmed by the soft light, we sat on the old wood benches, sang hymns and carols, listened to the Christmas story read once again from the Bible, and worshipped together silently for a while. When he was thirteen, Geoff was asked to sing "Oh Holy Night" as a solo. He practiced at home for days, and then worried when he woke up with a cold that day. We watched him stand up in the flickering shadows that night, start to sing tentatively, then gain confidence in his clear boy's voice, and manage to reach and hold the high note, his face lifted, straining, in the glow of candles held by dozens of Friends.

Two days after Christmas, my parents hosted my father's old school chums for their wedding anniversary. As she did for any party, my mother made lists of what to get and who would do what chores. Daphne and I vacuumed and scrubbed, set up extra tables in the living room, ironed the linen tablecloths, got out the wine glasses and plates painted with images of Westtown School. We peeled potatoes and baked cookies. Geoff set up the logs in the fireplace and helped my father shine the family silver. When the twenty or so guests arrived, dressed up and beaming, my father brought out the sherry and everyone gathered around the fireplace, sharing notes about children, telling favorite stories, asking us kids how we were doing in school, what we were interested in now. Like our Bryn Gweled neighbors and Quaker Meeting, this gang of my father's loyal friends felt like extended family who would care about us for a long time to come.

Into the Valley

In Bryn Gweled, we lived on Woods Road and our best friends were the Polsters, who had four kids, just three houses down, past the "High Woods." Geoff, Daphne, and I would walk through the dark of the looming trees each Sunday night for the Walt Disney movie on their TV, or occasionally on Saturday night for *Leave It to Beaver*. Besides owning a TV, they had goats and sheep, and raised baby chicks under a heat lamp in their living room. Their youngest child, Celia, was my sister's best friend and I was sure I was going to marry Tarp, their third child, or so I told him when we were nine, and he was helping me deliver the eggs I sold to the neighbors. Their second child, David, was Geoff's best buddy. Sarah, the oldest, was the artistic wizard who painted the mini-portrait of Grandma Troll, then sewed the bedding for Daphne's troll house. Tarp's name was actually Alan, but my father dubbed him Brer Terrapin from the Brer Rabbit tales he read to us at night. Geoff was Brer Rabbit, David was Brer Fox, I was Miss Mink, Daphne was Miss 'Possum, and my father was Brer Bear. Only "Tarp" stuck.

Geoff and David did everything together—lashed lean-tos and played Davy Crockett in the woods, built ice hockey goal cages and a tree house stocked with Playboys, wet the snowy sled run on our front lawn so it would freeze overnight, swam at the community pool all afternoon in the summer. They were inseparable—kept pajamas at each other's house, walked together to the school bus stop, beat the rest of us at Monopoly on snow days, and crafted birdhouses at the

Bryn Gweled
Pond.

workbench in our basement. If Geoff and David got rowdy inside the
house, my mother would say, "Take it outside, boys! Take it outside!"
And they'd streak off into the meadows or woods around us.

David's father designed their house in 1950 to be solar absorbent,
using Frank Lloyd Wright's concrete floors and hot-water pipes in
the ceiling to heat the rooms. It was more a huge shed than a con-
ventional house, but Geoff, Daphne, and I loved visiting. It smelled
sweetly pungent, of dirt and cooking and animals, which inspired in
us a sense of casualness and relaxation, as if no rules applied. True to
their philosophy of treating every living being as an intelligent, responsible individual, Norm and Betty Polster put their children on an
allowance and told them they had to figure out how to save enough
to buy their own underwear and socks. Often the kids couldn't find
the money or the underwear. One day we watched Tarp whizz down
our road on his bike, wearing only a bathrobe, cut-offs, and black
motorcycle boots. "Whaddayathink?" we asked each other. "Does he
have any underwear on?"

We felt like siblings. One summer our family came home from Maine and drove our big white station wagon, still filled with luggage and camping equipment, straight to the swimming pool. After we parked, Geoff was standing on the tailgate reaching up to get down the bag with our swimsuits from the roof rack, and suddenly there was Tarp, on his way to the pool, leaping onto the tailgate too. They whooped, and then hugged each other hard, not seeming to even realize they had never hugged before.

David was most famous for an evening at the Jersey shore when my parents took us to the drive-in movies to see *South Pacific,* which they had last seen as a musical on Broadway when they got engaged. Pajamaed and packed in the back of our station wagon, we kids rolled around and occasionally watched the big-screen scenes move back and forth between beach and close-up, dance and kisses.

The music swelled to the penultimate kiss on the beach. My parents watched, misty-eyed.

David leaned over into my parents' front seat. He must have been thinking about his and Geoff's sailing lesson that day. Staring attentively at the huge screen, he asked in his high child's voice, "Hugh? Is that high tide or low tide?"

After purposely missing a beat, my father said in a mock earnest tone, "Now David, I just don't know. I was looking at another high-water mark." And we all started giggling and jabbing at David until he finally got the joke.

Through David, Geoff began to learn about activism. David's parents were outspoken lobbyists. After the Supreme Court decided in 1962 that prayer in the public schools was unconstitutional, they lobbied against Bibles in the classroom. As Congress debated nuclear response, Norm, a physicist, was invited to Washington to testify on the dangers of nuclear fallout and radiation from bomb tests.

During duck-and-cover drills in grade school, David was the only student not to crawl under his desk—his parents had already taught him such actions were silly in the face of nuclear bombs that might drop on the air base down the road. One night, as Betty and Norm handed out leaflets, David and Tarp questioned a guy selling fallout shelters in the parking lot of a shopping mall. Inside the shelter, as the salesman demonstrated the little air pump which was supposed to provide fresh air, the boys asked questions like, "What will you do during the fire storm?" When he showed the food and water cupboards to the small crowd, the boys asked, "How will you survive down here for years?" Finally the salesman got angry and kicked the boys out.

Like us, the Polsters were Quakers. Several of the families along our road were early members of BG and Quakers—"the quiet power behind the throne" of the Homesteads, as a friend put it. Because pacifism was a tenet of both our Quaker upbringing and of Bryn Gweled, as children we were unaware that we held a minority point of view in the world at large. Nonviolence was something we thought everyone always wanted, as Geoff wryly noted in "A Christmas Thought," a poem he wrote in 1963, when he was twelve:

> "What do you want for Christmas, Sonny?"
> Says old Santa, big and funny.
> "A Mighty Moe is nice to have—
> Shoot down light bulbs on Christmas morn.
> A Tommy is nice, you see
> Shoot poor Santa in the Chimney!"
> All these war toys to celebrate His birth,
> The time when peace was to come to earth.

By junior high school, BG kids were voicing their liberal, Democratic views more publicly, particularly in class discussions of social issues, and occasionally Geoff joined in. But the majority of Bucks County students, like their parents, were white conservative Republicans. In 1964 David Polster's social studies teacher led the class in discussions about the Johnson/Goldwater campaign. David was the only student in the room to favor Johnson. He sat in class for the whole period with his arm raised, but the teacher refused to call on him. In the comfort of Bryn Gweled, though, for Halloween David and Geoff created, to great applause, a donkey they sewed from burlap feed bags and crawled into—Geoff wearing a donkey head, David bent over as the rump—and draped with a purple LBJ banner.

Occasionally a kid on the bus would call one of us a "commie pinko." When we asked our parents why people outside of Bryn Gweled thought we were Communist, they explained that Communist described the governments in Russia and China where the government owned everybody's land and they dictated how to live as a way of legislating equality. Perhaps, they said, these kids knew Bryn Gweleders owned the land together and that we all made decisions together about our common land, so they thought we were like Russians or Chinese. Or, they said, these kids heard their parents talk disapprovingly of our more liberal politics—we believed in government helping poor people, we believed in legislated racial integration, and their parents were perhaps more skeptical about those things.

More likely, kids saw we wore second-hand clothes, ate sandwiches with whole-wheat bread, or lived in handmade houses, and they judged such differences as odd, maybe even vaguely disgusting. Or, they saw the bus pick up the only Asian and black kids on our route. We did think of ourselves as distinct, and our parents encouraged it. They spoke of the Southampton powers who had made it hard for BG to get underground wiring, sewers, or some zoning break because they wanted to dissolve our community. We kids heard such comments

Woods Road Kids at the bus stop.

without understanding, but we took them to mean somehow that we were better, higher, special, and "they" were the unenlightened masses.

In the fall of 1964 Geoff was in eighth grade at the brand-new Klinger Junior High School, enjoying some heady successes. He was elected student body president and he hosted a conference of other SBPs around Bucks County. He played clarinet in the school orchestra and center halfback on the soccer field. In Industrial Arts class he spent his time designing, then making, the mold for a medallion of a clipper ship to celebrate the new "Klinger Clippers." Geoff's buddy, John Fesmire, helped him rally the rest of the class to make the medallions to sell as a school fund-raiser. In the spring, Geoff won first prize in the Science Fair for his study of hydroponic tomatoes and was invited to take it to the Franklin Institute in Philadelphia. At the end of the year, he received the American Legion Award for the second time, and then brought home the Yearbook that had his picture along with his "Message from the President." We were so proud.

But at the same time, Geoff was beginning to struggle with his status as the good Quaker boy. One day that year Geoff took chalk and scrawled "Fuck you" on the road by the BG pond. My father saw it later and mused openly about the various boys who might have been so crude. Geoff said nothing. That winter, his friend Bob Stahl was at the skating pond with Geoff when a bunch of older guys came by and started bullying them. Geoff got mad and made some kind of threat, like don't do this or there will be some kind of violence, and then he stopped and walked away, as if he were embarrassed by what he had said.

Then, near the end of the school year, as student body president Geoff was warned by a classmate that there was going to be a gang fight, and that a friend of Geoff's had brought a gun to school while others had stashed knives in a locker. Geoff was scared, knowing if he squealed, he could get hurt, and if he didn't, somebody else might get hurt. He talked to my mother about it, and with her encouragement, he finally reported the warning to the guidance counselor, who then confiscated the weapons and disciplined the students. His friend with the gun was suspended for the last two weeks of the year. Days later, a gang of boys pushed Geoff into the boys' room, wrestled him into a stall, shoved him to his knees, and crammed his head into the stinking toilet—the torture known among school bullies as "the deep six."

Because my mother kept her confidences with Geoff, I knew little of his travails. I saw only the diplomatic, talented Geoff, whose clothes I ironed every week, and whose advice I sought, even as I competed with him for approval and attention. But the Geoff I admired began to change, even to me, as he entered ninth grade the next fall. We irritated each other with almost helpless impulsiveness. He knuckle-punched my arm whenever he passed me in the hall. I taunted him with hollow bravado. I had no idea what was going through his mind. I only knew I was feeling keenly my inadequacy compared to him. That fall I followed him to the junior high school where he had been student body president the year before and a straight A student in the accelerated program. I was greeted with smiles of pleasure because I was his sister, and then just quiet acceptance when I got Cs as well as As and Bs in the program. And recently I had become obsessed with my twelve-year-old pudge.

One day as I collected laundry, I stopped in Geoff's room and saw a pair of his blue jeans rumpled on the floor. For years, I had seen us as similar in body, athletic and strong, even though in old photos I look thicker than he, "sturdy," people would say. The last time I had shopped with my mom, I had to find the racks of husky sizes. This was bizarre to me, and I couldn't quite figure out what was happening. Geoff was older; maybe his clothes could fit me. I slipped off my corduroys and picked up Geoff's jeans. Sliding a foot into a pant leg, then the other, I tugged, pulled the pants up over my knees, and then gasped in frustration as the waist dug into my thighs, unable to budge higher. Argggg, I cried, jerking them off and flinging them back to the floor. Hurriedly, I pulled back on my more ample girl-pants. I felt clumsy, dumb, and ready to bust something.

In that fall of 1965 it seemed tensions were rising everywhere, in continuing race riots and because of the conflict, as the newspapers called it, in a country I thought of as vaguely connected to where our Chinese neighbors came from. Geoff read the newspaper, and he heard boys talking about what their dads were saying about communism and the threat of it coming here. My father heard those comments too, but at first reserved his responses for my mother, after dinner, when they'd put the felt "cozy" over the teapot—the signal for us three that we now had permission to leave the table to do our homework and they could catch up on each other's day. One night I was reading in the living room, and heard snippets of my father's irritated voice.

"They say, 'Better fight 'em over there than in the streets of San Francisco.' Pure hogwash. They don't even have a plane that can get halfway to Hawaii."

My mother in her quieter voice was harder to hear from my sofa. She said something about the Gulf of Tonkin.

"It probably did happen," my father said. "Some U.S. Naval warships—what the heck, if you go into the theater of war, you expect to be fired on."

My mother said something about the South Vietnamese. I knew she wasn't defending the U.S. She was already cutting out clippings arguing about our involvement. With some of her women friends, I'd heard her talking, saying she believed it was wrongheaded, but information was still sketchy. She liked to try and see both sides of a situation first.

My father was more certain in his assessment, as usual. "That South Vietnamese government is as crooked as any government can be. We should never have become involved in this mess."

The next morning, at breakfast, we kids scrambled to finish our oatmeal while Dad read the paper. Suddenly he said, scowling, as if to himself, not looking up, "Good heavens, they're going to send another ten thousand to Vietnam. This will never convince them communism isn't right for them."

I glanced at my father, his frowning scrutiny of the front page, but was more concerned with finishing my cereal and getting my school-bag together. Geoff looked at my father intently, but because he was in a rush too, he didn't say anything. He knew David's family was already joining in peace marches and vigils against the escalation in Vietnam. But Geoff also knew our parents weren't marchers. They preferred more private ways of expression—letters to congressmen, AFSC clothing collections for victims of war, the occasional tense discussion after a board meeting they attended—my father at the Cheltenham Bank, my mother at the YWCA. At home, we were sort of in a wait-and-see mode.

Then, David was jumped by bullies at school. It was late afternoon and most of the teachers had left. Half a dozen boys came at him, taunting him about his pacifism. David froze, but told himself to stand his ground. Just as the first boys grabbed him and started pulling him to the floor, fists beginning to pound him, he heard the voice of the janitor, saying in a thick Eastern European accent, "Sooo, boys, Vat ist de matter here." The bullies looked up to see the janitor strolling down the hall, holding a huge pipe wrench. They raced off.

David believed he was stronger than those who were picking on him. Part of what protected him emotionally against the taunts and jeering was that his parents instilled in their children a sense of hope that they were doing something positive to make a better world. Perhaps because David's family actually DID do things to actively protest the wrongs of the world, this self-affirming confidence settled in him solidly. It was a confidence we would soon learn Geoff wished for, but did not feel.

By October, Betty Polster was getting death threats. As president of the Women's International League for Peace and Freedom she was taking public stands against the war. Geoff was reading the papers every day. One afternoon, he brought an editorial to my mother. It argued "The Right to Protest." He read a sentence aloud: "Those who protest government policies which involve us in war, which one believes to be wrong, are not cowards or anti-American—but are preserving our democracy." Geoff looked at my mother. "That's just the way I feel," he said.

He was thinking a lot about war and definitions of right action in the face of wrong or adversity. In an essay for school, he analyzed Charles Dickens's *A Tale of Two Cities*, describing how Dickens depicted different types of characters, and how he developed them in the story. Geoff was particularly impressed by Sydney Carton—how "he grew as a person from one who lacked motive and purpose in life into one of the most heroic of characters." Only later would Geoff's admiration for Carton's end seem cruelly haunting:

> Through synchronization of the characters and the plot there comes a tremendous apex of suspense which in my opinion, Dickens solved very well, considering the many loose ends he had to tie

down. The solution to the climax, Carton's execution, was not so much tragic as it was glorious as indicated by Carton's immortal words, "It is a far, far better thing that I do, than I have ever done, it is a far, far better rest that I go to than I have ever rested before."

Outside the safe haven of academic assignments, school was becoming complicated. As Geoff entered William Tennent High School that fall, his academically accelerated group of friends, who had been a cohesive group since fourth grade, were split up and mainstreamed among different tenth-grade classes. Instead of being surrounded by thirty kids who knew everything about each other, they now were mixed with kids a year older, whose names and attitudes they didn't know as well. Geoff's understanding of who he was came under increasing attack. In one class, during a discussion of the growing conflict in Vietnam, Geoff's teacher, whom he liked a lot, expressed a view in support of escalation. "We're fighting with one hand tied behind our back! The best thing to do is bomb Hanoi and get the war over with. We're just fiddling around!" Either in class or after, Geoff apparently voiced his own views against the war, and within days, he was punched in the hallway and harassed into red-faced silence on the school bus for being a "commie pinko coward."

Geoff's wounded outrage spilled onto the soccer field. During a scrimmage at school another boy did something—some cheap shot, or kick, or shove—and Geoff just lost it. He got very angry, and physically went at the boy. John Fesmire, playing beside him, remembered the incident mostly because it was in such contrast to how Geoff usually was—a very easygoing guy. "That was the only time I saw him that angry," he said, "and we had known each other since fourth grade."

Then, on November 2, Norman Morrison immolated himself on the steps of the Pentagon—protesting the war, burning his body into the minds of Americans of every persuasion. Defense Secretary Robert McNamara watched, horrified, from his window above. My brother stared at the photograph in the newspaper. He heard kids at school say the guy was a loony. But Geoff knew Norman Morrison was a Quaker.

The following week, on Veteran's Day, November 11, members of Geoff's Boy Scout troop joined other community groups like the American Legion in a parade and rally. It was a rainy November day and Geoff had studying to do, so when he didn't ask for a ride, my father just assumed that he didn't feel like going. My mother, on the other hand, said that the scout leaders had explained to the boys that marching had two purposes—to honor the dead, and to show their support for our government policy in Vietnam. Geoff felt he could not take part in that support, and he was worried that his failure to participate would cost his patrol points. He hoped his fellow patrol members would be somewhat appeased by the fact he had won them points a week earlier by scoring high on a knot-tying contest. According to one of the boys who did march, speeches were made at the end which excoriated those who were against the government's policy in Vietnam. They targeted Betty Polster, David's mother, as the spokeswoman for WILPF.

Betty remembered the Veteran's Day parade well. The local paper had written an article about her, describing the views of WILPF on the Vietnam War and other issues. The article was factual, not biased, she said, "but this would, of course, give the views of a pacifist and Quaker." She remembered the parade was sponsored by the local American Legion and that Geoff's scout master was involved, although she didn't know if he was a Legion member. Betty believed it was largely the scout master, not the scouts, who was applying the pressure to participate, and it may not have been a scout-sanctioned event. The parade, she said, was meant to "show that there were lots of red-blooded Americans despite what that awful Betty Polster promoted."

The parade and the condemnation of Betty were reported in the local Southampton paper, and Geoff read the story. He was well aware that the parade, encouraged by his scout master, was in part designed to put down his best friend's mom and her views. That weekend Geoff went to our Friends Meeting House to hear a talk on how to become a conscientious objector. Geoff had asked my father about the process and now he wanted more official explanations, even though he had four years before he would be required to register with his draft board.

At dinner Monday night we talked about Geoff's plans to visit our cousin Rick Thompson at Westtown School the next Saturday. Rick was in eleventh grade there, and since he and Geoff had always been peas in a pod together, he had called to invite Geoff to spend a night with him when Geoff came for his interview. We all assumed Geoff would start attending Westtown the following fall.

But the next day, Tuesday, November 16, Geoff came home from school and, alone in the house, he and I bickered—about what, I can't remember—until we exploded in unprecedented rage. "Fuck you!" I spat, using the word I had never said aloud before. He stared at me in shock. And then he slapped me, hard. No one in our family had ever slapped someone. I ran down to the basement, looked for some way to hurt him, saw his beloved workbench and grabbed his oilcan, squirting and showering slick, yellow goo all over his tools. Then I took off for the woods, into the November shadows and the embrace of damp air as I stone-stepped over the creek, trees reaching toward the late afternoon sky, hiding me from all human eyes and knowledge, letting me calm down, return to simpler sensation, far away from complicated emotions.

Two hours later, as the dark settled in, I returned to hear my father and brother arguing at the dinner table about what he would say about Thanksgiving for the opening of his Boy Scout meeting that night. My mother said nothing as I sat down late, knowing I had missed my job of setting the table.

"Why doesn't thee tell them about the history of Thanksgivings in thy families?" Dad said.

My brother shook his head dismissively.

"What? Is thee embarrassed by thy heritage? Thy mother's family settled in Maine when it was still part of Massachusetts. They've been celebrating Thanksgiving longer than any of these Boy Scouts' families. They might learn a thing or two." My father's voice got thinner as he wound up, saw Geoff wasn't buying it.

"Why, most of these families just got here—from Germany, and Italy, a generation or so ago! And now they're escaping the city out here, building up our farmlands." My father's disgust was barely veiled.

I heard his implicit "them" and "us." But these guys my father was dismissing were at school with Geoff and often came over to play—in the woods, down at the pond. The heritage that was a blessing to my father, a heritage that gave him a sense of belonging and of importance, seemed to have become a confusing burden to my brother. His desire to find a speech that pleased his friends, that didn't set him apart, was struck mute in the face of my father's tense enthusiasm.

Finally, red-faced, Geoff muttered, "They don't want to hear about my family!" and he jerked away from the table. He stomped up to his room and brought back the Scout Manual—announcing, tight-lipped, that he would read straight from the chapter about American holidays. "See," he said, pointing at the T of Thanksgiving on a page with diagrams of a cooked turkey. "How to carve a Thanksgiving turkey," he read. "It's a skill, no matter what your family. Nobody can laugh at that," he fumed.

He stuffed the manual into his coat pocket and left the house. In a few moments we heard his bike tires crunching down the gravel driveway. He would catch a ride as usual with his friend Paul Seelig, Jr., and his dad who was an assistant scout leader. That evening he arrived early at their house, and while he waited for Paul Jr. and Sr. to get dressed, he sat down and watched Mrs. Seelig as she ironed. She asked him how things were going. He told her his father hadn't let him march in that march last week and as a patrol leader he was afraid his patrol would lose points.

We will never know all that was said and done at that scout meeting. Based on various reports, my parents believed Geoff's patrol was indeed denied some points because Geoff hadn't marched in the parade. Then, one or more of the scout masters separated Geoff and sent him into a little room. The scout master or masters reminded Geoff that just two weeks earlier the Quaker Norman Morrison had taken his infant daughter to the Pentagon and set himself on fire as a way to protest the growing involvement in Vietnam.

"You're a Quaker," someone said to Geoff. "Would you do that? Give up your life to show how much you disapprove of our boys in Vietnam?"

An hour later, Geoff came home and told the babysitter she could go now. My parents were out learning how to play bridge so they could play with Geoff, since recently he had won a competition in the card game with a teammate from Bryn Gweled. But it was an unseasonably mild night and the roads were densely wrapped in fog, and they would be late getting home. Geoff came up to his room and I sleepily heard him start to take off his Boy Scout uniform, drop something onto his bed. Then I watched him pass my open door and I heard his footsteps go on down to the basement. I assumed he was going to work on his bicycle, which he was converting from one gear to nine. My eyes suddenly focused on the dark. Did he see the oil I had poured all over his workbench in my fury at him that afternoon? Would he know I had done it? Minutes passed and, tired of waiting for a response, I dozed off.

And then, from deep in my sleep, not far beneath me somewhere in the bowels of our house, a bellow came. My eyes flew open, slamming into the dark.

"Dottie! Get a Knife! Dottie!" My father's terrified yells hurled me awake.

Fire, I thought. The oil caught on fire. I hurt Geoff.

Scared, I slipped down the upstairs hallway, down the stairs to the kitchen, and was about to go down the basement stairs when my father bolted up from below and shoved me hard so I fell back on the kitchen floor. "DON'T GO DOWN THERE!" he yelled. "GO TO THY ROOM!"

I shot back up the stairs.

That's it, I thought. He knows I did it. I burned Geoff.

I sat huddled on my bed in the darkness. I heard my mother's strained voice on the phone. I turned on my bed lamp. I couldn't sit still. I went to Daphne's doorway. In the darkness all I could see was her curled shape. "Daph?"

"What's going on?" she asked.

"I don't know. Geoffy's hurt."

"Really?" She sat up fast, staring at me through the darkness.

I sat down beside her. I told her about my fight with Geoff and the oil and Dad's yelling like I'd never seen him yell before. We just sat there in the darkness, listening for some sound from downstairs, our hearts pounding.

A car crunched its way up our long gravel driveway. Somebody knocked at the door. I heard our neighbor's voice, and my father's, then my neighbor making some phone calls.

More waiting. Another long crunch on the gravel driveway. The front door opened again. I heard Dr. Williams's voice, usually calm, now tense. Footsteps down to the basement. I pressed my shivering body close to Daphne, who had curled again into a ball, her fingers stuck deep into her ears, trying to block out the fear.

Minutes passed. Silence. Then slow struggling footsteps up the basement stairs. Shuffling in the hallway.

I couldn't bear it. I crept down the upstairs hallway and peered around the corner at the top of the stairs to see down into the hallway below.

And there was Geoff. Just lying there on the wood floor in his Boy Scout uniform, his face pale, his eyes closed, as if he were sleeping, oblivious to all this attention. Dr. Williams leaned over him, his hands just lowering Geoff's ankles gently to the floor, and when he straightened his big body up, I saw under his raincoat he was wearing his pajamas. My father and mother stood near Geoff's head. We were all just silent for a long time. Dr. Williams asked to use the phone and as they all moved to negotiate around Geoff's body, I turned to find Daphne right behind me.

We hid in the closet doorway by the stairs. More waiting. More crunching on the stone driveway. Flashing lights through the closet window. An ambulance. The front door opened downstairs. Quiet voices talked as if by rote to each other. Shuffling on the floor again. Bumps and straining. The door closed. The ambulance crunched away down the long dark driveway.

My father came slowly up the stairs. He turned the corner to head toward our rooms and found Daphne and me peering at him like scared animals from the closet doorway. He pulled us both toward him, wrapped his big strong arms around us, and whispered with a hoarse voice into our huddled heads. "Geoffy ——." He choked, as if some vicious hand were ripping the air out of him. We stopped breathing. "Geoffy's dead." He paused, trying to get air down his throat again. "He strangled. On a rope." My father's tears streamed down, onto our heads. "He's dead," he said again. But the word sounded disembodied, as if he had never heard it before and he was trying it out.

I don't know where my mother was just then, but I imagine she was sitting collapsed on a chair in the kitchen. I cannot fathom her state of mind and heart at that moment. But I see her sitting at that round kitchen table where she had rolled pie dough and cut Christmas cookies and served sandwiches and dinners for five, and heard the day's news, and talked through difficult subjects, and just loved being the center of her family's hubbub. And now in one hour it was gone, ripped away, blown apart, destroyed, never ever to be reclaimed.

In a little while, our neighbor Wayne, the minister, came, and we—I remember my mother joined us now—sat on my bed and he asked what passage in the Bible we would like. I said Geoff's favorite was the twenty-third Psalm. Together we recited those words—"Yea though I walk through the valley of the shadow of death, I will fear no evil, for Thou art with me, Thy rod and thy staff they comfort me . . ." Words that suddenly meant us. Geoff. Now. This moment. This was the valley. The words were real, alive, palpable, and God was here, holding us up, leading us through, holding us . . . as we sat there in the soft glow of my bed lamp, unable to fathom . . . just feeling . . . what no words could express.

Our neighbor Anne came and said she would take Daphne and me with her for the night, so my parents could be alone. As I waited in the darkness near her car while she made last-minute plans with my parents inside, I looked up into the foggy November night and thought, well, maybe Geoff wasn't really dead yet. Maybe the ambulance took him off, and doctors were able to . . . It felt like a revelation, and suddenly I found myself whispering to God, saying, if He could just let Geoffy live, I would—. I tried to think of the worst thing I could do to myself. Suddenly I told Him, with deadly seriousness, I would become a Catholic nun.

Growing up Quaker, references to Catholics tended to position them as opposites to us. My twelve-year-old mind understood that Catholics practiced a kind of voodoo, they weren't allowed to think for themselves, and they had to rely on priests to talk to God. The implication was that Catholics were a bit lame; we Quakers were independent, intelligent, and spiritually evolved enough so we did not need a priest, or even a minister, to help us feel that of God in each of us. In my young mind, to become a Catholic meant prison, penance, a life of shackles to an arbitrary master. As I stared up into the foggy shroud of that November night, I actually saw myself in a burlap robe. I decided I was willing to pay that price for the gift of my brother's life.

Around midnight that night, the phone rang loud and startling at the house of Paul Seelig, Sr. It was the scout master. He had just gotten a call from the father of Geoff Taylor. Geoff had hanged himself. He was dead. His parents wanted the Boy Scout leaders to get to their house right away. Paul Sr. was stunned. He drove the half mile to our house and found in the living room my parents, several neighbors, and the minister from the church where the scout meetings were held. He and the scout master told them all they knew.

Just three hours earlier Paul Seelig, Sr., had dropped Geoff off at his house and he had seemed fine. He did not seem troubled. As far as Paul Sr. and the scout master knew, nothing odd had happened at the scout meeting. Geoff had done a good presentation on carving a turkey. All the patrols had done their different projects as usual. If anything had happened to upset Geoff, it might have been among the kids. My father would hear a different story later—that the Seeligs brought Geoff home early, leaving his bike at their house, because he was so upset, "a mess" in fact.

The next morning my best friend Allie was standing at the bus stop when Tarp ran up and spouted his powerful news. "Geoff Taylor hung himself in the basement last night!" But nobody waiting at the bus believed him; he was known for the dirt behind his ears and for being the class cutup. The news flew through the corridors of William Tennent that Geoff Taylor had died. Someone said suicide. Someone said, "Maybe it was an accident." Someone mentioned the Boy Scouts. Someone said, "Well you have to admit they were pretty rough on him last night." Geoff's soccer buddy, John Fesmire, called his neighbor, who happened to be the chief of police. He stood at the pay phone in that school hallway and heard his neighbor's familiar voice confirm the impossible report of Geoff's death.

That day, the local Southampton paper ran the story:

Student Leader
Boy Found Dead In S'hampton Home

A 14-year-old Southampton youth was found dead by his parents last night in the basement of the home.

Jeffrey [sic] Taylor of 999 Woods Road, described by neighbors as a "very sensitive" youth, was found by Mr. and Mrs. Hubert

Taylor at 10:35 p.m. with a rope around his neck. The rope was tied to a beam in the ceiling.

After the parents cut the rope they applied artificial respiration to the boy.

Dr. Gomer Williams Jr., who was called to the scene of the mishap, said the youth died of asphyxiation about a half hour before the parents found the youth.

Bucks County Deputy Coroner Burton Decker ruled the death a suicide.

Taylor, a ninth grader at the William Tennent High School, Johnsville, was wearing his Boy Scout uniform when discovered.

He was described by school officials as an excellent student.

Taylor was a youth leader of the First Day School of the Southampton Friends Meeting and president of last year's student council at Eugene Klinger Junior High School, Southampton. He was also a member of the soccer team.

He is also survived by two younger sisters.

Neighbors at the home this morning said the youth had been disturbed in recent weeks over the bombings by U.S. planes in North Viet Nam.

The *Philadelphia Inquirer* ran a brief obituary as well, and after citing the time of the memorial service, noted that "In lieu of flowers, contributions may be made to the Friends Peace Committee, Phila."

When my buddy Allie got home that afternoon her mother met her at the door. All she said was "Geoff has died and Beth is coming over." Her mother couldn't explain much, and then there I was at the door. On a regular school day at the Bragers', five to six o'clock was the allotted TV time, and it was always *Three Stooges* and *Superman.* I walked into their TV area and sat down beside Allie. Together we just stared at the flickering images, silent, parallel in our utter incomprehension. I stayed for an awkward dinner where no one knew what to say. And then Allie's father took me home, and she burst into tears.

In the days following Geoff's death my parents tried desperately to piece together his story. He had left no note. The clues they managed to gather seemed to point toward Geoff being the victim of harassment at school and at Boy Scouts for his views against the war, despite the denials of some. By the time David Polster showed up at our door for the first time since his best friend had died, they seemed already to have accepted this explanation. My mother hugged him for a long time, standing in the hallway, crying. "Don't let this happen to you," she said.

Later that afternoon our parents suggested we take one of our cherished strolls down Woods Road, to get out of the house, to try to walk away from the nightmare, hoping it was all a bad dream. We walked quietly, together, down the old school path past the meadow, feeling the cool air, noting the clear sky, but feeling every familiar detail was surreal. Even the old weeping willow tree seemed shrunken into silence. We turned onto the road, still quiet, walking four abreast, barely aware our bodies were moving. Suddenly we heard the labored gears of a bus and we froze. In our fog we hadn't thought to look at a clock. The big yellow school bus came around the traffic circle and started heading up toward where we stood in front of our meadow. That school bus was Geoff's, and all those aboard had been part of his daily life leading up to his death. Mom and Dad told us to turn around so we did not have to face the bus. We turned, stared at the grass, felt the hot stares as the bus went by—they had seen us turn around. I felt embarrassed, confused. Why did we have to turn around? What were we hiding? Or hiding from?

On Friday, November 19, we sat silently as my father drove our car quietly into the winding driveway of the Abington Friends Meeting House. We moved slowly past stately pine trees, barely aware of the cool blue sky above. We turned into the parking area and suddenly we were staring at a black hearse. My throat squeezed shut. Numbly, my father parked the car, and we walked, as if under water, pushing against a heavy tide, toward the Meeting House. In front of it stood a long, yellow school bus. No one was outside now. We started to walk past the long black hearse, but stopped, irresistibly, and looked at its dark windows with a stunned, uncomfortable disbelief. In there was Geoff. Geoff! We willed ourselves to push on, into the hushed embrace of the grand old building.

It was a Meeting House I knew by heart. Built of Pennsylvania light-brown stone over a hundred years before, the long porch wrapped around its window-lit comfort within. Long wooden benches sat one behind the other looking toward the facing benches where the elders sat. A few sturdy beams down the middle of the room reminded us of how, in earlier years, Quaker men and women saw their spiritual lives as separate, even if equal. My father's sisters married there, and in the sweeping lawn behind, dotted by simple, low, white headstones, one of those sisters, her baby, and my Grandfather Taylor were buried.

Now as we walked in, an old friend waiting in the hallway gently and without speaking led our family into the large meeting room. It was packed. Hundreds of people on all sides, and in the gallery above—kids, high school kids, not in school now but here, for Geoff. We were amazed, surprised—so buried in our private horror of the last two days that we had no idea this many people even knew. We walked in front of all those faces toward the first row where space had been saved for us. We sat down together, and fell into silence, tried to center down, find that place within that is calm beyond all feeling and thought. I could not find that place.

Mostly I remember being unable to stop crying, and gripping someone's hand very hard. A pamphlet inscribed with the twenty-third Psalm and a brief inscription in memory of Geoff was handed out to each person who came. A woman stood up—as anyone may do in a Quaker meeting—and quoted the Bible. "Blessed are those who are persecuted for righteousness sake . . ." Another woman spoke about the sacredness of all life, including one's own, saying if we are to bring peace, it must begin with each one of us.

A man stood up in the balcony and began to speak. It was the scout master. He said something about how, in any religion, parents must be careful not to teach their young too rigid an understanding of their faith. Heads craned and murmurs rippled through the room. What was he trying to do here? Blame my grieving parents for teaching Geoff the values he held? I heard intense whispering and then bodies moving, trying to muffle their disturbance. The scout master was surrounded and escorted out of the Meeting House.

Others spoke, and then, as the service was almost over, my father rose slowly, like a tired old man, and turned slowly toward the packed gathering of friends, family, Boy Scouts, and neighbors. He tried to say something, then cleared his throat, and started again. But he just stood there crying, for what felt like a long, long minute. I had never seen my father cry. "Do not be embarrassed by my tears," he finally said, his voice gravelly and choked. "I am not ashamed of them." He was holding a piece of paper in his hand and he said, "I didn't know that Geoff wrote much poetry, but I just found this among the papers he saved from seventh grade." My father's hand shook, and he cleared his throat again, so he could read Geoff's words.

> There's something about fall that stirs within me
> A feeling, a wild feeling of wanting to be free.
> I don't know why for sure, or what the cause may be;
> All I know is this . . . I wish I were free.
> Free like the wild, honking geese, bugling overhead.
> Free like the flaming sugar maple with colors gold and red.
>
> It's not as if I'm a slave for life,
> With life all full of grief and strife.
> But I just wish when mornings are cool
> THAT I DIDN'T HAVE TO GO TO SCHOOL!

I found no consolation or illumination in the cheer of that poem. We lapsed back into silence. Then our family filed out of the Meeting House and down the cemetery path to a tree under which a canvas had been laid, and Geoff's casket upon it. We stood there, mute. Somebody read a biblical passage, the cemetery caretaker spoke quietly to my parents, and I thought about how inside that casket Geoff was lying there wearing the blue and red madras shirt and khaki pants I had ironed for him on Monday. He was supposed to be wearing them in school this morning. But instead, in my mind's eye, I saw his sleeping face, just as I had seen it on the wood floor of our hallway three nights before. And then we walked dumbly away, back into the reception room of the Meeting House. There were lots of people, but all I remember was trying to hug one of my cousins. She just stood there, paralyzed, not knowing what to say. Like all of us.

Gentle Boy?

Why did he do it? Anyone who knew Geoff wrestled with that question. He didn't fit the stereotype of a troubled teen, or a loner with no support or dreams. He liked people, he slipped easily into leadership roles at school, in the Boy Scouts, and in our Quaker First Day School. He enjoyed doing schoolwork as much as competing in soccer, or playing hard in the summer. Girls said he treated them better than lots of other guys at the time. When I called them thirty years later, friends like John Fesmire, Rocky Tinari, John Stevenson, and Bob Stahl all remembered only the pleasure of fooling around and working with Geoff. Each said something similar to what Paul Seelig, Jr., said. He didn't remember anything seeming wrong. And, at that age, he said, they didn't analyze anything. They were just friends—they played together, went to Boy Scouts together, they just liked each other. "I knew our beliefs were different," Paul said, "but it didn't bother me. We never talked about the war and Geoff never complained about pressures or anything. I just remember coming over to your house and being welcomed by your mom and dad, and liking your community—it was unique, different, fun—just nice and friendly."

Bob Stahl was a patrol leader with Geoff in Boy Scouts. By chance, he could not go to the scout meeting the night Geoff died. The next day, when Bob heard the news of Geoff's death, he was incredulous. "I just didn't believe it. I didn't understand. I felt some guilt, too, because

I didn't go the night before, and maybe if I had been there, I could have helped him. But I'm not even sure anything actually happened. I heard from other people that his explanation of carving a turkey went very well."

Bob didn't remember any talk of Geoff being punished for not marching in a Veteran's Day parade. "There was never a punishment for not attending these things. Lots of kids didn't show up for one thing or another. We were always honoring whatever holiday it was—like Thanksgiving. But if you couldn't make it, you never got points taken away."

Paul Seelig, Jr., was the only friend of Geoff's who was at the Boy Scout meeting the night Geoff died. He didn't remember anything. He did remember that his father, an assistant leader, had been worried about Geoff because "he wanted to jump in and join in on everything, and yet at home he was being told he can't or shouldn't do stuff." What that stuff was is unclear. Their troop focused mainly on camping and pioneering skills, not on any paramilitary training. Bob Stahl remembered the leaders might occasionally refer to their backgrounds in the military, but only casually—they might say something like "This is a knot I learned in the Navy; it's most useful for such and such." But, said Bob, it was never a heavy-handed reference.

To many Bryn Gweleders, though, including my father, all Boy Scouts were seen as too militaristic, beginning with the rules for uniforms, details like brown socks with black shoes or black socks with brown shoes. Geoff was the only boy from Bryn Gweled who wanted to join. Like his father, who liked hunting even though simplistic definitions of Quakers would judge him an anomaly, Geoff too would be his own kind of Quaker—he would like Boy Scouts because he loved camping and learning outdoorsman skills, and he would ignore the occasional militaristic aspects and the disapproval of his friends at home. Or so we assumed.

Janet Schroeder, an older neighbor and Friend, supervised Geoff as he ran First Day School opening exercises. Soon after his death, she wrote an essay about him. She too saw Boy Scouts as militaristic, and, like most Bryn Gweleders, she presumed most choices were political. So she encouraged the view that Geoff's suicide was a political act. She asked, "Was this the case of a boy who had for a long time had the courage to refuse to go along with the crowd when he felt it was wrong, but could bear it no longer?" She quoted his admiration for Sydney Carton's noble sacrifice in *A Tale of Two Cities* and asserted the view shared by many of our neighbors:

> Nothing in Geoff's life had shown him to be the kind who would give up because he couldn't take it anymore. Some of us who were closest to Geoff believe he was rather one who, though perhaps confused over the difference between giving one's life (as with Sydney Carton in *A Tale of Two Cities*) and taking one's life, like Norman Morrison, he was seeking a way to make deaf ears listen.

Whose deaf ears? The Boy Scout leaders? The bullies? His father? For months, in sad conversations, friends and family asked questions about the Boy Scouts, talked about who knew what when, pondered my father's strong personality and our family's Quakerism, reconsidered Norman Morrison, wondered was Geoff secretly mentally ill, and if not, what if anything could have made a difference.

There was also the supposition that Geoff was maybe playing with knots, and he simply blew it. "We were always playing with ropes as kids," Bob Stahl said. "Down at the pond, out in the woods—probably more than we should have." Indeed Geoff liked tying nooses on his plastic cowboys and Indians. When he studied the French Revolution, he made a realistic foot-high model of a functioning guillotine, with a razor blade welded into soft lead, a carved-out head catcher, and a decapitated soldier-doll with blood painted on the torso. But, Daphne said, "It was just PLAY; it was what we did—out in the woods with our little stick forts!" Nonetheless, David Polster remembered in the months before his death Geoff played with ropes and knots and taught David how to tie a noose. Was he trying out a real noose on the beam in our tool room? Had he climbed up on the mower to see what it felt like to put his neck in it, just out of curiosity? Would a straight A student who loved all the rules of safe camping do that? Or had he been preparing for this moment for a lot longer than any of us knew?

Disbelief led all of us through helpless steps of query and conjecture. I buried myself in my room, and one day I suddenly wrote an essay about "The Rope that Killed My Brother." My parents visited a well-known psychiatrist in Philadelphia. He said, "You'll never know why. Never. All you can do is go home and love those two girls more than anything—and love anyone they love too."

A year later, my father and mother asked the Boy Scout leaders to visit them again. Paul Seelig, Sr., remembered, "Again we went, and the room was filled with neighbors, and again your father and mother asked what happened, and once again, no one had anything that could help." My father remained suspicious of their reticence: "After everybody had had their say privately, the general reaction was to clam up because you might get yourself in trouble."

Bob Stahl remembered my parents asking if they could come over and interview him. He was nervous, but finally, a year after Geoff's death, he and his parents let my parents visit. "I can't remember all of it," Bob said. "But I do remember one thing your father said was just 100 percent wrong, way off base—that I had promised to help Geoff that night, but I wasn't there. After that, I avoided them. I didn't buy what they were implying. And I felt badly because I really did not know what happened. Your parents couldn't accept it either, and they were trying to blame people. I can't say they were wrong to do it. I have a sixteen-year-old son now, and if he killed himself, I'd feel the same as they did. For a long time they were upset with anyone who had been near Geoff that night."

Because no Boy Scout remembered anything negative happening to Geoff, or to anyone in general, one wonders if it was just a lone leader who isolated him, unbeknownst to other leaders or boys. But how then did someone hear a boy say, "You have to admit, they were pretty rough on him last night"? Did a myth evolve purely from enough people hearing Geoff worry about losing points, even though he perhaps had nothing to fear in actuality? Did Geoff's own anxiety, hearsay, and my parents' grief and paranoia just concoct a comforting story of a child martyr? Or, has one of those Boy Scout leaders taken the truth of that night to his grave or the oblivion of lost memory?

I asked these rhetorical questions of Allison, my buddy from childhood, who became a well-regarded journalist at the *Boston Globe*. Her response was immediate.

"Oh something happened, alright."

"How can we know?"

"We can't in the factual sense. But I just know from having been in Girl Scouts there then. There was such a desire for conformity. I was the only Jewish girl surrounded by all those blonde—. I didn't think of it this way then, but it really was like Hitler youth. One girl told me flat out to shut up when we were singing because I couldn't carry the tune. It was nothing overt, but I felt ostracized. I quit."

"But if all these Boy Scouts have only fond memories . . ."

"Maybe they didn't see. It could have been something subtle, some comment that Geoff magnified. You know how teenagers are. It might seem like not much to someone else, but to you it's huge, and painful, a big deal. I'm sure something happened."

David Polster said his mother remained certain of her memory too: "Geoff was publicly humiliated and ridiculed, and this was not hear-say."

The prevailing assumption by Bryn Gweleders that Geoff had been a victim of blind-sided militarism was the view of our cousins, too–on both sides of the family. As my cousin Rick Thompson said a few years after Geoff died, Geoff's choice was an "ultimate witness" against the war. But many people who knew us less well believed Geoff's tragedy was more personal than political. No explanation seemed without a doubt. Paul Seelig, Sr., probably spoke for most people outside of Bryn Gweled when he said, "We never saw Geoff's suicide as political. We saw it as a terrible family tragedy. We heard rumors, like maybe he was having troubles at school, but we didn't know. It was just a terrible, awful waste."

Bob Stahl noted there were two or three other suicides in their class in the three years after Geoff, including a friend of Geoff's. And he said, looking back, he wonders if the pressures of their accelerated school program exacerbated whatever personal problems each of them was having. There was a lot of peer pressure to excel, Bob said. "We were doing a year's work in two-thirds of the year, so you ended up a year ahead of your actual grade level. Even in summer we had reports to do, and I just had a real hard time with that. It was summer! I ended up getting a bad attitude about the program. I don't know; maybe Geoff was having his own pressures that way too."

Noel Hill, Geoff's classmate and friend from BG, thought the schoolwork was not the problem. She did remember they were all taking the PSATs the day after Geoff's death. But she didn't remember any particular worry about the exams. "We were used to tests! We were always taking them!" In her mind, Geoff's death is still a troubling mystery. She never bought the Boy Scout and Vietnam story, or the playing with ropes story. "He was so articulate—he wrote poems, essays. If he meant it to be political he would have said or written something! And he was such a good outdoorsman, he would never have 'slipped' while playing with knots! Geoff never did anything mediocre or halfway. He made extraordinary drawings—I always thought he would have done something artistically. He just had too much depth, and he was too smart to just give in to some one event." She concluded, "It had to have been some complicated larger moral quandary having to do with 'who am I?'—the question any fourteen-year-old is asking."

That's why, she said, she sometimes wonders if he was just "maxed out" by my father, by "trying to carry the Taylor placard"—the banner of Quaker high moral duty, excellence in academics and athletics, and honoring family history. As another friend noted, Geoff was "signed up for college the day he was born"—Haverford, the embodiment of the family placard. I think of various friends and family who said over the years that my father, and to some extent my mother, just "lived for Geoff." And I think of neighbors' views of my father. He could be erudite and charming, but he could also be "a tough customer"; he could be "gruff." He could entertain them with historical and personal anecdotes, but, particularly after Geoff died, he could also yell at someone over an infraction of community rules, or "grill" them at monthly meeting over some issue, like putting a new roof on the community center, or some other expenditure.

Being true to the teachings of his religious heritage, my father often said, "You just don't hit people." But, on some level he understood that he had been born with a combative nature, and it had never molded well to Quaker censorship. Even without hitting, his words and personality could be harsh. This paradox confused us. He spoke the history of good Quakers, but he by nature could not act it. My mother, raised a Baptist, was taught to accept the fact of wars, but she had in her some deep sense of Christian generosity that came out in kindness and pacifism that seemed effortless. As my father said of my mother's pacifism, "She acted it, breathed it, lived it much better than I ever could." Somehow these tensions–conflicting messages about what did it mean to be human and a good Quaker, a pacifist, a man–all seemed to collide in Geoff in November 1965, scorching his soul until he erupted in a spectacular, volcanic meltdown.

The Shadow
of Death

I knew, even as a twelve-year-old, that my mother changed the night Geoff died. Once or twice, after Daphne and I had gone to bed, I heard her weep–harsh, wrenching sobs, bursting up from the kitchen or living room, as she tried to keep us from hearing. Then, I think, something deep inside her just went dead, turned off forever. She didn't stop her daily doings, but she lost the energy, or the confidence, to cope with Daphne and me at times. Once, when I lay sulking in my room for too long, she came in and put a book beside my bed, said, "You (she did not say "thee") might find this helpful reading." It was one of her college textbooks, on adolescent psychology. And that was the extent of our discussing whatever problem I was having. Then, when I was in ninth grade at George School, the Quaker high school near our home, she visited my English teacher, who had responded with great tact to a journal assignment in which I had written about the night my brother died. Apparently, my mother filled her in on our family, and then said forthrightly, "I can't be the mother Beth needs right now. If you can just keep an eye on her, give her any extra attention, I would be grateful." Dottie Coppock said she understood, and after that she started talking with me after school about anything at all. I had no idea my mother had visited her, but in many ways Dottie saved me during those sad years, and she was one of the reasons I would become a teacher.

Daphne was ten when Geoff died and utterly confused. "I had no sense of what was happening," she recalled. "My brother had died and I felt more a fear than a loss. That he would never walk in the door again was too abstract for me. I kept waiting for it all to be over and for him to return. But I knew he wouldn't. The sadness around me created an ache deep inside that felt like a knot and I wanted to walk away, play with pretty things and build little dream worlds with trolls and friends."

The hardest part was seeing Mom so sad. Daphne remembered watching her burst into tears as she sat on the love seat in the living room with a few friends who came to try and console us. "I remember going up to her and putting my arm around her, saying, 'That's OK, Mom.' Somehow, I thought I could make her OK. It was the start of a long road of trying to be a good child—not wanting to hurt or upset her, wanting to bring her joy, wanting her to be so proud and happy about me, wanting to be that good girl, do no wrong, not let them down."

But at the same time, Daphne was frustrated by our mother's transformation. "On trips into Southampton that first year, Mom was hard to deal with. Seeing young people about Geoff's age she would turn to us and ask 'Do you know them? Who's that? Who's that?' I remember screaming inside, wanting to tell her to 'Shut up, look at me!!!! Look at me!!!!! Think of me as much as you are thinking about Geoff.'"

Every aspect of our lives seemed changed. Daphne had been a happy fifth grader at the public school nearby. "Although I had felt differences, being both Quaker and living on a homestead, with my schoolmates I had always felt accepted, safe, happy, and proud of my family history," she said. "With Geoff's death this all went. Life carried a weird color to its landscape and nothing was ever normal again. Every act, every new thing, rite of passage, accomplishment was tinged with this distinct color or pallor. Darks were very dark— night a rough time."

Two weeks after Geoff died, Daphne and I went back to school for the first time. I stared straight ahead as I climbed the school bus steps and kept staring beyond heads as I searched with my peripheral vision for a free seat. Finally I found one and slipped in to stare out the window. So far so good. And then the inevitable happened. A huge stage whisper from a boy two seats in front of me to his neighbor: "That's the girl whose brother killed himself!" And all heads turned as I whooshed my nose right to the windowpane and felt my pale cheeks blush embarrassing heat. A month later our parents enrolled us in the Quaker school nearby, and Daphne and I left behind the democratic richness, and threat, of the public schools.

Soon, Daphne's dark nights erupted in horrible nightmares, with snakes crawling, hissing, and snapping at her from the foot of her bed. My parents moved her bed into my room, and I lay there in the dark, missing my privacy and hating her: If somebody had to die, why couldn't it have been her? I loved my brother; I missed him with a depth of pain I couldn't describe. It didn't matter that he had begun to punch me in the arm 'til I bruised. It didn't matter that he had seen my competition with him as a pain. It didn't matter that he had slapped me the afternoon before he died, or that I had tried to destroy his workbench afterwards. Now, in death he was only his good traits—smart, funny, creative, and amazing to remember. The idealization of my brother that my father had always encouraged was now in full bloom. In contrast, my sister was whiny and spacey and IN MY ROOM NOW.

As kids I had thought she was cute, and then I had seen her as a pain when she complained I was too loud making airplane noises as she practiced her piano, or when my mother asked me to watch out for her, or finish a chore for her. She always seemed sweet and unorganized, her room a mess, while I took pride in knowing every inch of my neatly arranged desk and closet. More painful, I resented her easier affection with Geoff. They were the oldest and youngest—the standard-bearer and the mascot. And they were simpatico, similar in nature. I was the in-between—the responsible one to the "baby," and the dark-horse "also ran" to my champion brother. Now, as he held my parents' attention even in death, Daphne and I were left, barely acknowledging each other, disoriented, robbed of our places in life–she no longer a baby, me suddenly the older, supposed to lead the way, but lost in the darkness of my own grief.

It was harder to see the changes in my father. Besides the pall that shrouded each of us, he still went to work, came to Meeting for worship with us, and took care of our property, just as he always had. But his law practice suffered; he just couldn't muster the energy to keep up the pace he had been working. Only with his closest old classmates and friends would he let himself cry. And sometimes with my mother. For a while, they struggled in their marriage. As we traveled by train across the country to see cousins the Christmas after my brother's death, I noticed my mother was refusing to speak to my father, at least for the duration of the trip. Only once in that year did I hear them fight, behind the closed door of their bedroom, her words muffled, his voice rising finally, incredulous, "What? Does thee want a divorce?" But that was it. Whatever they needed to do to accommodate each other, they figured it out. As my father's sister Marge said, "I don't know how your father would have survived Geoff without your mother."

Another responsibility my father let go during this time was the care of his childhood home. Brooklawn—where we kids played with an ancient rocking horse in the attic, wandered the lush flower garden tended by our Granna Taylor, and waded in the stream, trolling for mica, staying cool. Particularly after his mother died, two years after Geoff, my father stopped thinking carefully of that old farmhouse in Cheltenham; he found tenants and let them do as they would, until the stone walls literally began to crumble. Some of my cousins were irate that he had let this fine historical building deteriorate. Eventually a couple would buy it and restore it to its historical health. But my father could not face it. Somehow it represented the core of something— a legacy, a plan, an inheritance—that had been irretrievably lost with Geoff. Or, perhaps, he just said to himself, it's a house, it'll survive, I'll get to it, after I take care of business here at home.

At home my father's emotional turmoil translated into more rigid and irritable social control. He was still able to charm, compliment, and tell a good story. But more and more he was also critical. He snapped at my mother more often about chores or plans not executed right. And we girls needed to work on our flaws. In his eyes Daphne was always too timid; she needed to get out there and make that call, make something happen! She could still hear him years later, she said: "Little girl, Thee's GOT to learn to not be so shy." Or, she wasn't applying herself well enough at school: "Daphne, Thee has GOT to learn to listen in class! Thee can't stare out the window and daydream all the time!" To either of us: "Honey, I wouldn't say this in front of other people, but . . . (thee would make thyself prettier if . . . ; before we visit the cousins, I hope thee'll . . .)" His eternal comments to me: "Boys won't like it if thee . . ." (I needed to use more tact, tone down the salty language, walk down the stairs like a lady, smile more!) We growled inside, or in a few years we took off to the woods for a cigarette, alone or with friends. But we obeyed.

The year after Geoff died, to distract her pain, my mother took a job to get her out of the house. Former colleagues asked her to organize the fiftieth anniversary celebration of the American Friends Service Committee, and she was gone, out to Haverford College, four days a week. I prepared dinner each night, and looked after Daphne more. I had already taken on all my brother's chores. I mowed the lawn, carried out the trash, and built the fires on the hearth. While I had been a fair to good student before Geoff died, at a new school I now got straight As. We all tried hard to just do the right thing all the time; as a severed family, we limped through each day—careful, sober, and raw.

At thirteen, I felt very old, as if the elderly lady I was biologically destined to be had suddenly pushed through to the surface of my soul overnight. I couldn't see her in my soft pubescent body, but I could feel her knowing, her resignation, her acceptance. Little things didn't bother me as much, and if something wasn't working out, I had no trouble saying "OK" and walking away. Around this time, my mother mused one day, "Beth, you always seem to have a good sense for just how much effort is needed to do what's expected." "Umm," I nodded, noting that more and more she was forgetting to say thee, recognizing she had just named something new in me–a kind of efficiency, a desire not to waste effort or go beyond what was necessary. It was true. With Geoff gone, I didn't feel so competitive anymore; every action and goal was purely to do my part in the family, or to satisfy my own pleasure in something done well.

But some nights, lying in bed, I felt a penetrating loss of connection that terrified me. It was as if a rift in the atmosphere had cracked open and all natural elements–air, oxygen, gravity–had suddenly departed, leaving me without sense–of my body, my surroundings, my life. Suddenly I would realize I was losing touch. And I would force my conscious mind to wake up and shake off the dread, pull myself back to here, now, in my bed.

I stared into the dark grays and shapes of my room and felt the wavelike roll of what life was now–no longer rooted to firm ground, but uncertain, unpredictable, easily upended, in a minute, overnight. I had always loved the word "suddenly"–its feeling of excitement, its promise of adventure, fresh and new. But overnight it had become death, fear, dread, crash, loss, worry. Now, all the thrill, optimism, and possibility of that favorite word were irrevocably intertwined with anxiety and caution. On the rolling waves of my dark nights, I thought, if life is suddenly death, if all that was normal, stable, comprehensible, was ripped away in a night, turned into nothing in one night, then what? What does any of it mean—any task, or day, or expectation? How do we know anything we do or feel or believe in is real? Why should I trust any of it? What protects us? What holds us up?

During the day, I watched my classmates irritate each other, or my teachers ask for volunteers, or Daphne do her homework, and I felt like an outsider looking in–calmly detached from usual conversation, activity. When I had to go out in public, more and more I took my camera. Now, I loved it not only for its metallic smell, its logical mechanics, but because it gave me permission to be mute. I didn't have to speak or engage; I could watch, I could hold on to what was, and not open my mouth. I know I did speak–whenever I was asked a question, assigned a verbal response, or needed in a task. But I felt silent, watchful, wary.

The only certainty I knew was in my memory–images, various scenarios, of Geoff, the Polsters, me, Daph, my parents, nights by the fire on the hearth, walking in the woods, on the beach, painting at the workbench, sledding down the hill, swimming in the pool–together, alive, happy. I'd hear an old song–the Huntsmen, "Who ya goin' to run to, oh brother man . . ." or I'd see geese fly overhead, and my mind would zoom back into scenes so vibrant and colorful, I'd lose myself in the midst of chores, conversations, car trips, as my mind played over and over again the movie of what had been. Those stories made sense. They followed a certain, clear logic that helped me steady myself, find solid ground, if only in my imagination.

And then, one day, the numbness erupted in a well-planned, weirdly thrilling ritual. It was a Saturday and my father had asked Tom Ambler, his closest Quaker friend, to come over with a sledgehammer. Pounding began in the basement. I walked down the stairs, and there they were–two men who had known each other since boyhood, now in their fifties, still fit, stripped to the waist, sweating, and swinging huge iron sledgehammers hard against the walls that had formed the tool room where my brother had died. Tom had two sons. Neither man said a word, their mouths grimly set. Smash! . . . Breath. The hammer swung again. Smash! . . . Breath. Dust swirled. Smash! . . . Breath. Smash! Smash! . . . SMASH! Within hours the room, the hallway near it, were no more. Just a pile of rubble and shattered wood. Within months another Quaker friend remade the open space into a finished basement with lots of light, helping Mom and Daphne and me to reclaim it for art projects and coolness in the summer heat. We added a couch and a new TV, offering the comforting, if mindless, distraction of *Gunsmoke,* or *The Beverly Hillbillies,* or *Get Smart.*

During that time, our friends missed us. If you ask them all these years later what was the hardest part of Geoff's death, they'll say that besides not understanding at all why he did it, they lost Daphne and me, their best friends and playmates. Allie and I had been Tarzan buddies swinging on the vines in the woods, or playing Barbies, or skating with the boys' ice hockey team, or playing octopus every summer afternoon in the pool. She took me to Friday night services at her synagogue and I fell in love with the musical chants of the cantor. But after Geoff died, we never played together again. As she remembers, I got whisked away to private school, and she was jealous because in ninth grade she had to go to William Tennent, the high school where my brother had been. She remembers once I took her up to my high school, but I was "distant, cool. You had come to blame the students at Tennent for having been so horribly crass in teasing Geoff," she said, "and I felt, since I was at Tennent, you included me somehow in your condemnation."

One night, a year after Geoff died, the Polster family walked together up through the woods, sat in our living room by the fire on the hearth, and explained they had made a decision. They were pulling up all roots and leaving for Canada. Betty and Norm would teach at a Quaker school in Argenta, British Columbia, and the kids would go to school there too. They were looking for a society more akin to their beliefs. What that meant and they didn't say: after David was accosted by bullies, after Betty was excoriated in public, after Geoff had died, they felt warned. I sat there on our hard couch feeling speechless, unable to think of anything appropriate to say. I looked at the faces of Sarah, David, Tarp, and Celia, each of us expressionless, as if stunned, reduced to being good soldiers, accepting whatever came at us.

One of the few people who could cut through the sorrow during those first years of our new life was my cousin Rick Thompson. At Geoff's memorial service he couldn't speak to us. But while he boarded at Westtown, he visited our family faithfully, helped my father with repairs around the house, and enjoyed long talks into the night. We were charmed by his handsomeness and warmth, felt energized by his drive. And he transformed my father. Together they stretched out their legs before the fireplace in the winter, or settled into the wooden lawn chairs on the terrace in the summer, and they talked for hours— sharing off-color jokes and favorite New Yorker cartoons, making respectful fun of teachers and old Quakers they both knew at Westtown. They talked about Haverford College, about liberals and Democrats, about Johnson's troubling choices, about Grandfather Taylor and how he set the family standard for good works, tough moral business sense, and high-profile campaigning for the Democrats.

They told stories about Geoff, too—remembering fishing at the New Jersey shore, adventures in the woods, some funny comment. In Rick, during those visits, my father had his son back. Rick knew this, and he always showed respect and affection for my father. His own grief at losing Geoff was probably somewhat appeased by those nights of loud guffaws and occasional tears. Between them there never had to be the father-son tensions that my father would have had with my brother, and which Rick sometimes had with his own father. During the weeks of his Senior Project, when he stayed with us and worked with a welder in the next town, Rick would jog the three miles back to our house late in the afternoon, and I would sit and watch him eat half a jar of peanut butter at our kitchen table. Then he went to work on the troll house Geoff had made for Daphne, carefully replacing the electrical lines and bulbs that had died. For Daphne and me, he was a big brother in the house again, and we loved it.

It would take a few years for Daphne and me to become friends. Off and on, in high school, we began to recognize each other as if from afar. We moved through classes and chores, family gatherings and vacations at the beach, where we soaked up the sun and took long, quiet walks. But mostly I buried myself in the stories of other people's lives in soothingly long novels and she drew quiet pictures of hippy-dressed friends in stages of solitude. During the school year I earned good grades, acted in plays, photographed, and played field hockey and lacrosse–"a nerdy jock," according to my best friend Soo. Daphne filled walls with drawings, made clay pots, sewed and embroidered colorful peasant shirts and mini-skirts, baked Euell Gibbons's acorn bread, squeezed dyes from berries, stewed dandelion wine, and made great dinners of rice with vegetables from our garden.

Often I would clean up after Daphne's grand meals. Working together in the kitchen—she creating, me cleaning—we chatted, asked each other questions, and there came a day when I suddenly remembered I had once hated her, and I was floored by my ugliness. How could I ever have hated this kind, gentle person who used all her great energy to just give things to people—food and paintings and pots and weavings, all with their own distinct Daphne-characteristics? It was as if, after these years of walking heavily under that dark, murky water of grief, unable to hear or see each other well, we finally realized that the other had always been right next to us, and now we never had to be so alone ever again.

Daphne and me posing back-to-back in my photo studio.

Sister

For my first real date—on my sixteenth birthday in 1969, dressed up in tight bell-bottoms and an almost see-through blouse—a neighbor boy drove me to arty New Hope, where he bought me ice cream and a lead sculpture of the Trojan horse that held incense sticks. I knew he wanted to give me my first real kiss, but on the way home I finally burst into tears and blurted, "I'm really sorry, you're very nice, but I have this problem where every guy I see I can't help but compare him to my brother, and, well, he was just . . . well, no guy could ever . . . well I'm just screwed up about it I think, and I'm sorry, you've been so nice, and I don't want to be unfair . . ." He pulled the car over and kissed me anyway, and I'm grateful.

Geoff seemed to live in every action, every thought. Who he had been, the loss of him, and what he represented lived like a constant presence in our house, lurking in every chore or habit of a day. This did not feel like a choice; more like a shroud, light and fluttery, or a scrim that had descended, separating us from the rest of the world. And from our past. My childhood was gone; I understood I was now different, set apart, benighted and scarred by our horrible knowledge. All I could do was follow where that knowledge led me.

Because in my mind Geoff had been a good Quaker and a casualty of the war in Vietnam, for years after his death it was comforting for me to try and be as good as he might have been—organizing moratoriums at George School, standing quietly in peaceful demonstrations against the war, doing guerrilla theater with Vietnam vets in the streets of Philadelphia and Washington. I was earnest, well meaning, and sure of my mission. Life was gritty and sad, and each boy I read about or knew who left for Vietnam as a soldier, or for Canada as a resister in exile, or for prison as a draft card burner or war protester, seemed to be my brother crucified, again and again and again. I became so focused on the stories of the young men around me that I would write my application essay for college arguing that the choice about Vietnam each man made affected not only him but every woman in his life.

Trying to bring our boys home was not just a political act for me. It felt deeply personal. No family should know what I knew—what it was to lose a son and brother to war. Or, a mother, father, sister, aunt, uncle, or grandparent—as the evening news constantly reminded us, in grainy black-and-white images of panicked, tearful Vietnamese or Cambodians, running down dirt roads or huddled near burning thatch-roofed huts. Moratoriums and demonstrations offered a constructive response to death, if only symbolically.

My parents joined my friends and me in our efforts. They funded my trips to Washington, stood in vigils with us—listened as drivers yelled, "Get a job, you commies!" On our kitchen table I now found brochures–I.F. Stone's Weekly, the Central Committee of Conscientious Objectors, the War Resisters League. I felt proud of my father as he helped young men face the difficult decision about the war. He took me along when he visited our neighbor Chris, imprisoned at Allenwood for resisting the draft, and he testified for Mike, who felt he was a conscientious objector but since his family was not Quaker, he wasn't sure he could convince the draft board in Doylestown. My father sensed that Mike's Friends Meeting in Wrightstown, sitting in the middle of conservative Republican Bucks County, was nervous about supporting Mike's C.O. stand. So my father stood up with him in a Sunday meeting for worship, reminded the Meeting of Quakerism's pacifist philosophy, and said that it was our duty to publicly support Mike. They did, and my father drafted the letter that helped convince the draft board that Mike was the C.O. he said he was.

In October of 1969, my junior year at George School, I went to Washington for the National Moratorium Against the War. I had heard recently that Butch Geary, a boy I loved watching as he led us in the 4-H Club pledge on summer Saturdays, had died in the spring fighting as a

Marine in the war. I hadn't even known he had gone. Ensconced in my Quaker world, it hadn't dawned on me that I would ever have to know someone actually lost to battle. Now I saw his wide smile in my mind's eye as I walked the grassy mall and stood near veterans, some with no legs, or missing an arm–with wheelchairs or canes. I studied their faces, trying to see—what, I don't know, but thinking, they've been there, they've seen it, and wanting to comfort each one of them.

The Washington Monument speared the sky in the distance as I wandered among demonstrators dressed in jeans and work shirts, wearing black armbands, holding signs exhorting "Vietnam for Vietnamese," "Quakers for Vietnam," "Silent Majority for Peace." We sang "The Star Spangled Banner" and "We Shall Overcome." Dr. Spock, the man I associated with my mother's well-worn copy of *Baby and Child Care,* yelled into the microphone, "This War is a total abomination! It's crippling America! It must be stopped!" The crowd roared approval.

Then, suddenly, the mood broke. Screams and yells came from atop the hill behind us as we faced the stage. The crowd seemed to push against us as if the middle were retreating, and suddenly we could see clearly a band of protesters dressed in black, running down the slope, holding aloft huge North Vietnamese flags. "The Weathermen," somebody said. And I was scared. Their rude, out-of-control violence swept aside the peaceful recognition of sorrow and nonviolence. It would be their picture that made the papers the next day, but I knew that most of us there saw them only as the school bullies who had found one more way to upstage the peacemakers. Peacemakers like Geoff. And like Butch Geary. Or was he? Butch had seemed to me like an older version of Geoff—tall, lean, freckled round face, a great grin, and a leader with smarts and humor. I realized that even though I had had a crush on him, watching him run 4-H meetings, I didn't know him at all. He had seemed a peacemaker. But he had gone to this awful war. I didn't have a clue why that handsome young man had to be dead.

The lottery for the draft sent some of my friends into a tense time of trial. If the draft number for their birth date was high, they stopped worrying. But if their number was low, they felt suddenly forced to consider paths they hadn't imagined a year earlier. It was easiest to continue on the track toward college and take a student deferment.

But sometimes there was a nagging guilt. Were they a coward if they refused to go to war—or if they gave in and went to a war they knew was wrong? At the time, I believed the tension of being patriotic while also being opposed to the war was the noose that strangled my brother. By 1970, enough American soldiers in Vietnam had come home to condemn their own actions that most young men I knew decided they would be fools to go toward the war even as a medic. If they were uneasy with a college deferment, they went into the Peace Corps or did alternative service.

Tony McQuail decided he couldn't follow any of these scripts. The son of my mother's former roommate, Tony had grown up on an old farm near Downingtown, west of Philadelphia, and we had visited his family on summer evenings or the occasional Sunday. His mother Ginny, like my mom, had found Quakerism her preferred berth. Like us, Tony was raised with little TV, lots of reading aloud, chores like mowing the lawn and cutting firewood. His father instilled in him a love for the land; his mother taught him to work for social justice. He knew he wanted to be a farmer one day.

During our high school years—Tony at Westtown School, me at George School—we began to write letters back and forth. We described our moods and questions about life, shared our pleasures

Geoff and Tony McQuail.

in photography and acting, complained about the "traditionalism" of our school rules or the apathy of our peers, philosophized about different kinds of friendship, or the wisdom of Ghandi and Buber. When we wrote about the draft or the war, I invoked Geoff's memory as reason for my worries and hopes for Tony's future. Our families continued to visit, and once, when I stayed with cousins and friends at Westtown, I watched him perform with great aplomb the title role in Faust. By then I flirted with the idea of joining Tony as a farmer's wife someday and I was head over heels when he sent me a poem, "To Five Ladies." I didn't care that he was a ladies' man. Like my crushes on some older neighbors or acquaintances, he was one more smart, kind, charismatic guy who helped fill that deep black hole in my heart just a little bit. Tony was not too much older, out of reach, or gone; he was an appropriate heart-throb, and my vulnerable longings for love latched onto his cavalier affections with grateful pleasure.

By his senior year Tony was one of the more eloquent public speakers against the war among young Philadelphia Quakers. As the student body president at Westtown, in the spring of 1970, he organized and spoke at rallies against the war in the nearby town of West Chester, and publicly announced his refusal to register with his draft board. He knew he could easily avoid Vietnam by being a conscientious objector, but as he helped other young men in his Quaker Meeting explore the choices open to them, he became convinced that the draft was a tool of the war trade, that it created artificial support for the war, and he could not cooperate with it. This wasn't an easy decision. In fact he was torn apart by the possible consequences. Partly he was fighting the fact that he had always been a good kid—top of his class, active in his community, a Life Boy Scout, cocaptain of his wrestling team; he took rules seriously and only broke one if it proved untenable after earnest, rational scrutiny. But finally, in his letter to the U.S. attorney general, he asserted what many young men were realizing: "I do not believe that I can consciously support a system which forces others to plot and participate in the destruction of other human beings."

At Quaker Yearly Meeting that March, in the old, darkly cool Fourth and Arch Philadelphia Meeting House, I watched as Tony rose from the balcony seats and spoke passionately and thoughtfully, asking whether as a Yearly Meeting we were living up to our Peace Testimony as actively as we might. I finally managed a moment alone with him that day and wished he didn't have to whisk away so fast to one of his many acquaintances—or girls. Even as a teenager, he was seen as a leader whom at least one teacher openly described as someone destined for greatness. Looking back, Tony said he could also be seen then as "pompous—a pain in the ass" by some who heard his confidence as conceit. But to the dozens of friends and family with whom he kept up a rich, detailed letter correspondence, he was a clear, engaging voice among peers who often felt at sea.

Weeks later, I sat in my favorite clearing in the woods near George School and wrote in my journal, dating it May 5, 1970.

> I feel quiet . . . empty–because I am not eating today . . . Nationwide student strike because Nixon has pushed 3000 more soldiers into Cambodia–and because 4 students were killed yesterday at Kent State University in Ohio. I'm not fasting to prove anything to the world, just to myself. One doesn't make a point by killing oneself by fasting, by immolation, by hanging oneself . . . We, all, are needed to fight together against what is morally wrong . . . and first we must fight against getting bogged down in pessimism and apathy–hard, very hard . . . It's so easy to feel helpless . . .

In each death I felt the ghost of Geoff. But as the horror of deaths by random violence or confused accident mounted, I had begun to realize that in contrast Geoff had made a choice–and he didn't have to. I no longer was seeing him solely as a victim. Without feeling anger yet–it was still easier to feel only compassion and sadness for him–I knew that any form of self-laceration was not only wrong, but illogical—a self-defeating perversion of hope, or of true activism, which was meant to celebrate life by protecting the civil rights that sanctified that life. Likewise, Norman Morrison's self-immolation was the antithesis of my understanding of God's way, of Christ's teachings, of Quaker faith. He was "mad" in my mind—not courageous—and he may have been partially responsible for my brother's lapse in sanity.

Tony, on the other hand, was living out the next step of what could have been Geoff's life. In him I felt hope and control, ambition and moral confidence. He was a successful embodiment of the Quakerism and family values that Geoff had failed to survive. In Tony I could love a familiar constellation of admirable traits, keep them alive–in a body I could actually talk on the phone with, write letters to, and hug.

After Tony refused to register on his eighteenth birthday that spring, an FBI agent came out to his family's farm in Downingtown just after Tony graduated from Westtown. Tony was working the assembly line in a sawmill and recalled coming home tired and frustrated by his day in the world of "industrial tedium" to the man in the dark suit waiting for him. They agreed to disagree on what were one's obligations to country and to God. Surprisingly, the agent said he would not arrest Tony if he promised to register by the fall. Tony agreed. He understood the agent was taking a risk by letting him off the hook awhile longer.

A few weeks later Tony came down to our cottage at the beach. I was ready to be swept off my feet. He did kiss me, there by the waves in the windy darkness lit up by the moon. And then he said good-bye. He was going to Canada to become a farmer and to live in a society that felt less alienating. I stood there on the cooling sand, and looked through the moonlight at his piercing eyes, his rich reddish-brown beard, and those soft lips I had just enjoyed with totally different expectations. I had no doubt he would do everything he envisioned. But all I could feel at that moment was the familiar chill of loss. I shook it off. "Of course," I thought. "What did you think—that he too would actually stay?"

I returned to my senior year full of plans and determined optimism—playing field hockey, editing the Yearbook, working as an aid at a mental hospital, applying to colleges. I felt propelled by energy and confidence. But there were times driving alone in the car that fall, an illicit cigarette in my fingers, the darkness enveloping me in my womb of thoughts, when songs on the radio would softly pull me back to Geoff. "Leader of the Pack," "He Ain't Heavy He's My Brother," "Love Is Blue." In the privacy of a dark Pennsylvania winding road where no one could see me be weak or bad or emotional, I would let the grief well up, let it spill over, let myself weep and rage and pound the steering wheel. Afterwards I would feel purged, lightened, ready to get back on track.

One winter night I discovered that whatever needed purging in me dug much deeper than a good cry could touch. Daphne and I had invited friends over to Tobacco Road when our parents were gone. Good dope was passed around and Daph and I decided, what the heck, why not. It was explosive stuff. We sat around the fireplace, staring at the flames, listening to each other's surreal comments through the echo chambers that our brains had become. Daphne went upstairs and I found myself rising, walking toward the flames, then bending down and trying to crawl in, searching for something inside those shadows and flickering lights. A friend took my arm, led me back to the sofa. I sat there and felt myself begin to slide down a long, slow wave, pulling me down, sucking me down into a dark, wordless place of dread and horror. I could hardly breathe. It was so cold. Something was about to happen. It was so, so dark. Something had just happened. Something awful. Where was Daphne? I felt my way up to her bedroom and found her huddled in her bed.

"It all came back, Bethy."

"I know, Daph." I sat down beside her. "We don't have to do this again."

I understood now, there was a monster rift in my brain. I knew why it was there and that there was nothing I could do about it. What I could do was respect it, keep it deeply hidden, contained, so it could never swallow me again.

As spring came and longer days began to lighten our moods, I found myself enjoying a real, here-with-me-now boyfriend. Bogdan had grown up on the Lower East Side of New York and had come to George School with the help of the Boys' Club. He was a soft-spoken, gently humorous guy who created huge ceramic pots in the art studio and drew complicated abstract sketches. We shared the same birthday, a year apart, and somehow, despite differences in upbringing, we felt at home with each other. He liked my wilder moments, called me his "freaky chick," and introduced me to the exquisite pleasures of careful but exhilarating making out. He was my "street boy," who carried his switchblade in his back pocket even when he wasn't in the city. And the respect for elders he learned in his three-generation Polish-American home went over well with my parents. He helped my father around the house, dug the hole to plant our Christmas tree, and hung out with my mom at the kitchen table. When he told my father he saw two moons on one of our so-called night walks, my father bought him glasses. One spring day, I took some of my savings from a summer camp job and bought us a helicopter ride to buzz our friends–all waving on the wide green lawn of George School below. With Boggy I discovered what was possible, the comfort and pure pleasure of just having a good time with a guy, unburdened by the weight of grief.

Then came May Day of 1971, which would become famous for violent protests including logjams that shut down Washington for days. Leery of the crowds and the potential for violence, I decided to go down the week before with a group of Pennsylvania Vietnam Veterans Against the War to do guerrilla theater in the streets of the capital. We were supposed to enact for the lunchtime crowd what a raid on a village looked and felt like, complete with machine guns and blood, and bodies tossed like potato sacks. Another girl and I were "victims" to four vets dressed in fatigues, their crush hats drawn low over their eyes, throwing shade over a scraggly mustache or nervous eyes. I tried hard to chat with them as regular guys, feeling again, as I had at the October '69 Moratorium, a confused sense of apology.

The enactments were frightening, rough, and fast. A photograph in the *Washington Post* shows my body, dressed in work shirt, blue jeans, and desert boots, flung into the street, a puddle of blood on my belly and a soldier standing guard above me, his plastic M-16 held tightly on alert, his eyes scanning the horizon, waiting. After awhile he would reach down and take my hand.

"It's OK, you can get up now." He pulled me to my feet, and my head was sore and dizzy.

I glanced at him. He was crying. Surprised, I touched his arm. He shook his head and backed away.

"It just got—real," he said, his voice tense.

He looked down at his gun. The plastic was cracked. He looked at me with shock in his damp eyes. "Did I hit you?"

"It's OK. I'm OK," I said.

He stood there staring at the plastic gun. One of the other vets came over and put his arm on the soldier's shoulders. "It's OK, Dennis. All over."

I watched their green-uniformed backs walk slowly away, deeply aware of the unalterable chasm between us.

The next day our group went over to the Winter Soldier Investigations being run by the Senate Foreign Relations Committee. A young man sat at the panel table and coughed slightly into the microphone. He stared straight ahead at some dot on the back wall, and he spoke in a quiet, almost inaudible voice.

"I lied about my age to get in because I wanted to go in before the war was over. I didn't want to wait. So I lied." His stare at that back wall did not waver. His cheeks flushed in the glare of lights, and his sandy hair fell down over his lean face. He seemed shorter and slighter than everyone in that room. But he had been in Vietnam. He was my age.

"I'm here because I seen things I know are wrong. Things I know aren't always talked about or in the newspaper." He was almost whispering now, reciting a litany of horrors into the microphone.

He paused and stared at that wall. A senator asked him a question.

The young man didn't even glance at the questioner. "It's not orders. It's just what we do."

Somebody asked another question. The soldier seemed to clench his teeth. "We don't always know who is enemy. When we do we can't shoot 'til the order comes from the rear. I seen buddies blown up in that time."

Another question. The young man still stared straight ahead. "It's not what I thought it was going to be."

I looked at that young man, who looked like a boy, across the hot, crowded senatorial room, and I thought how out of place he must feel, trying to explain what he had seen and what he understood now to people who seemed kind enough, but who were looking at him like he was a june bug on a windowpane in winter. Like my soldier on the street the day before, I couldn't imagine him ever being who he once was again.

Later that afternoon I stood in a small crowd outside Congress, watching as hundreds of Vietnam veterans hurled Purple Hearts, Silver Stars, and Commendation medals over a fence that had been set up to discourage this event. A father blew taps for his son. A mother clutched her son's flag. A vet said into the microphone his wife was divorcing him because after today he would have no medals for his son to be proud of. "It means NOTHING now!" he cried. "It meant something once, but that was before I woke up!" Each vet said something about his medal, how he won it by being lucky, or how it belonged to a friend who couldn't get there today. But mostly each said he wanted to be part of this public testimony because of his grief and rage and end-of-the-line determination to end this war right now.

When our little band of Vietnam vets and Quakers left Washington, we saw buses beginning to pass us as they came down for the traffic-stopping May Day party that was being advertised as the protest to end all protests. My mind and heart were full of the quieter testimonies—the soldier Dennis, that boy staring at that Senate wall as he said publicly he is here but he has died already. All I wanted, despite the obvious impotence of symbolic protests, was to help these young men to hang on. I wanted to let them know that someone was listening, to finally be a good sister.

Personas

During high school vacations, my father began to take me on jaunts—to courthouses, to visit shut-in clients. As we traveled together in his new Volvo—"Quaker gray with sexy red interior," he'd wink—I began to realize there was an unspoken assumption that in the absence of Geoff, I would carry the intellectual mantle of the Taylor legacy, maybe even be a lawyer. Doors were beginning to open for women in traditionally male professions and my father's sister offered to introduce me to a law professor who was recruiting young women. Dutifully, I studied some legal torts from Civil Rights battles, debates over integration whose stories I knew. But after the first three pages of "Whereas"es and "Wherefore"s, I knew this use of the English language left me cold, drained the blood and emotion right out of these searing tales. My heart was in literature—the characters, images, and histories that had pushed the boundaries of my own understanding, showed me ways in which others loved, coped, fell, resurrected, endured in different times and cultures.

Soon I was off to Smith College, drawn to my mother's New England, interested in what a women's community could be like, intrigued by the five-college consortium. On buses that wound through wide, flat tobacco fields and neatly lined orchards, then around the camel humps of the Holyoke mountain range, I traveled to art classes at Mt. Holyoke, a history course at Amherst, a literature class at U Mass. With a friend at Hampshire, I kayaked through the white waters of the winding, tree-lined Connecticut River. I found my friends at Smith in the co-op house, the art department, English seminars, and the Quaker community around Mt. Toby Meeting, high in the leafy hills northwest of the college.

In the grand rooms of the old brick dorm I enjoyed the rituals of sherry and tea, of formal dinners and holiday parties where we composed poems or songs for each other–vestiges of an arcane but endearing concept of gracious living. And I liked the discipline of studying hard all week, undistracted by boys, even if at times I felt overwhelmed. One night during exams, I sat in the library holding the Norton Anthology of English Literature and I panicked as I tried to memorize, analyze, and interpret all of English literature. Suddenly I was certain I had made a big mistake; I was in way over my head here. I stared numbly at the words of Keats's "To Autumn." Slowly, as I reread for the tenth time, "Season of mists and mellow fruitfulness, Close bosom-friend of the maturing sun," I began to hear my father's voice reciting those lines, and the terror I was feeling dissipated as I was swept back to my childhood kitchen table when the words of a great writer were made living and human by the familiarity and affection my father gave them. I passed the exam, but I began to see that the English major was limiting–mostly male and British authors at the time. I would move on to American Studies, using the frames of history and sociology to understand American literatures of all kinds.

In the distance, the war continued to rumble. One day, a friend showed up in my dorm after going AWOL from the Army in Texas. I had met Joel in the summer, working for my father's friend, Tom Ambler. While he figured out what he was going to do, he put his stinking Army boots in the hall outside my door and I brought him leftovers gathered as I cleaned dishes for my job after dinner in our dorm's kitchen. I knew eyebrows were raising up and down the hall. One girl had said recently, in a bemused, sweetly Southern accent, "Beth, I just don't see how you can talk to me as nice as you do–I mean, my daddy being a General in the Army and you being a pacifist and all!" Now I worried how much she might intuit about Joel's status. Finally Joel decided to go home to Pennsylvania and get help from Tom, who served as an official Quaker minister. Two weeks later my father called and said Joel had been arrested while hitchhiking. The police found a bit of marijuana on him, did a background search, found he was AWOL, and delivered him to Fort Dix in New Jersey. Joel had called Tom who had called my father, and the two of them drove over to see what they could do. Dad said Joel's head had been shaved, he had been stripped naked and thrown into solitary. Tom and my father managed to get Joel out on a dishonorable discharge, which in Joel's mind was better than heading back to boot camp or Vietnam.

On Friday nights I worked with Frances Crowe, a grandmotherly draft counselor who helped young men from U Mass and Amherst decide what path they wanted to follow as they faced their draft notice. If they wanted to defend their conscientious objection, we role-played their hearings before the Springfield Draft Board, or helped them construct appeals before the state board in Boston. Most of the young men who came were Catholic. I was amazed at how familiar they seemed to me—not the boorish, mindless stereotypes of my childhood presumptions, but philosophical pacifists who were struggling with the dilemmas raised by their own church tradition: What was the definition of a just war; if this was a just war, could they justify killing another when the Ten Commandments bade them not? They found solace in the teachings of Catholic labor organizer and pacifist Dorothy Day, the antiwar stance of *The Catholic Worker*, and the civil disobedience of Catholic priests like the Berrigan brothers. The young Catholic men were an education to me, and I was quickly smitten by one of them as we rehearsed his interview with the draft board. One day I asked Frances why she thought I could be so drawn to a Catholic when I had grown up thinking they were everything I was not. "Well," she said, "I guess no matter what the differences, you each share a deep sense of conscience. Neither of you can be free of it."

Off and on, I wrote letters to my cousin Rick Thompson, who had continued checking in with Daphne and me as he went through college. Now he was working in Washington, D.C., as an intern for the Friends Committee on National Legislation, drafting reports on Indian legislation. During spring vacation, he brought his girlfriend, Linda, to visit us at Tobacco Road. As we joked and told her family tales, she responded with a story about Rick courting her at his apartment with dinners of rice—rice appetizer, rice entrée, rice pudding. I watched Rick laughing, delighted at her dramatic narrative, and I knew he had found the woman he could marry.

But the following August Rick came to say good-bye. He was going to Vietnam to work for the American Friends Service Committee in their hospital at Quang Ngai. Again he warmed us with his humor and teasing gibes. We sat on the terrace in our usual semicircle of wood-slatted chairs, enjoying the cool of the lush, green evening. He said he had registered as a C.O., but as he draft-counseled others he began to see his choice as just a privilege, unfairly offered to the few. Although he had sent back his draft card, he felt compelled to face this war that was defining our generation, do something that might actually help the healing in some way.

As I listened to him, I watched the fire flies signal from the darkening gloom down by the blackberry bushes and garden. Rick sounded so logical and clear, but this was complicated.

"Isn't thee scared?" I said.

"Sure! I'd be stupid if I weren't. It's hard on Mom and Dad—the risk I'm taking. They thought I was going to go to graduate school."

"It must be hard with Linda," my father said. "We so enjoyed meeting her—a lovely girl."

"That's the hardest part," Rick said. "But she's being a real trooper, just a saint about it."

We all sat silently a bit.

"This is an extraordinary opportunity," Rick finally said. "I just can't NOT go."

We nodded, felt his excitement, tried to smile, gazed out into the shadowy trees of the summer night. And then the next day he was gone.

Over the next few months Rick wrote us letters describing life in Quang Ngai. He fixed everything—tools, machines, electricity, the VW bus, and he studied Vietnamese so he could negotiate and run errands for the team. He battled cockroaches and spiders in his tiny bedroom, coped with frequent stomach illnesses, created cassette tapes for family and Linda to help him stave off the loneliness of being the only single staff member. He flew to Saigon for errands and to escort patients whenever he could. He loved the adventure of it all, but was depressed by the wards full of children without limbs. Even though it was the fall of 1972, when peace talks and "pacification" were supposedly slowing the war, bombs and artillery fire shook his room at night. "The war that is winding down at home is in full swing here," he wrote. "The center has more patients than ever now."

That fall I stood with ghostly, white-faced demonstrators at the gates of the Westover Air Base, protesting the B-52 bombers as they took off for Vietnam. But my attention was being drawn to a different kind of activism. A professor invited me to join a new seminar described as women's studies–reading Margaret Mead, Simone de Beauvoir, Sylvia Plath. When we discussed our own lives, I proudly described my mother's example, her years as a teacher and administrator, marrying late for her generation, her closeness with longtime women friends. The other students were older and all talked about various struggles with lovers. I spoke of the boys I had known, the ones who seemed to "get it," the ones who were a throwback to barbarity. I tried to sound articulate in my new feminism, but I felt out of my league. One woman declared we should follow Germaine Greer's dictum and taste our own menstrual blood to truly embrace our bodies. I was more worried about my inability to be as sexually "liberated" as these women seemed.

The summer before, I had met Stephen, a fellow counselor at a camp in Vermont. He asked me out one night after he saw me decline the dope being passed around a late-night campfire, impressed that I seemed unfazed by being uncool. On our nights off we drove for beers at a local bar, canoed out in the middle of the lake, skinny-dipped at midnight. We felt older than the others, and were not surprised to discover sorrow in each other, his father having died young. He was gentle and calm, offering comfort and intimacy. I wanted it too. But when the moment came, I froze; I was not ready. In part I heard my mother's voice–"sex before marriage spoils it," and my father's voice–"I ask thee not to derail thy education by getting pregnant." But mostly I was just scared. Of what, I wasn't sure. Being hurt, being left again. Why did it seem so easy, so casual for others? On some deep, deep level I felt bound by my upbringing and trauma to a life right now more like a nineteenth-century novitiate.

Penitently, I poured my energy into studying and a political action group. We lobbied for the lettuce boycott, showed films on the war in Indochina, organized a weekend on women's issues, created an open dialogue for lesbians on campus, and started an alternative newspaper.

Portrait taken of me during my freshman year at college.

Mom and Dad, Bowdoin College, Maine.

At home on spring break I chastised my mother for giving up her career for marriage; she said she felt like she didn't know me anymore. I argued with my father about the definition of rape; he told me I seemed mad at the world. I realized we were all a bit right. It was time for me to lighten up, take a break from all this angst. So I retreated to the life of books, decided to live the high life at Oxford for the summer, where I could read Shakespeare, Virginia Woolf, and D. H. Lawrence on their own turf.

In June I flew to Europe and was hitchhiking through Switzerland before heading to England. At the base of the Jungfrau, Switzerland's highest mountain peak, I sat down on a bench surrounded by green grass and wildflowers and pulled out a letter Rick had just sent us from Quang Ngai. It began with an oblique allusion to Geoff's choice of suicide, reminding me how intertwined Rick's own decisions were with losing Geoff. He said he had just finished reading *Craig and Joan*, "a powerful, unsettling document about two young people who took their own lives after the first Moratorium in 1969. It was disturbing and yet so close to compare others' responses to such an ultimate impact." Rick described his feelings more frankly than ever before. Whatever plans he had vaguely made before Vietnam, whatever view of himself he held dear, they were gone, and he was in limbo, trying to figure out the consequences of so many changes so fast upon him. I studied the photograph he had sent—of him, leaning against a white jeep with the AFSC star painted on its door, his arms crossed, his smile almost grim now. On a Swiss postcard, I wrote him a note, musing at the beauty in my life right then and the contrast to his life in Vietnam, thanking him for his letter, asking him to tell me more, telling him I loved him.

At Oxford I looked forward to reading and walking, wearing long dresses and sipping tea. And I longed, in a chaste kind of way, for a lover to sweep me off my feet. Xavier responded from the start. On the first night I got trapped into an argument with a renowned professor who baited me with the proposition that living with women must be a bore. As I challenged the don on his assumptions and our debate drew a little crowd, Xavier stood on the sidelines and grinned, entertained by my seeming fearlessness. The next weekend he took me to London for dinner, then a concert, grabbed my hand to waltz me down an alley, helped me climb over the iron gate when we returned too late to the college. The next week he made a picnic so we could watch boat races on the Thames and took me after a play to meet its star, Vanessa Redgrave–"Why not!" he said. He charged into my room late one night and drunkenly crawled into bed, shushing me to just let him sleep. Another night we snuck into the darkened chapel, lit candles from the altar and placed them in a circle of light, fending off the stony gloom as we shared soul secrets that could have been written by Lawrence. As the dawn began to lighten the high arched windows, he took my hand and we walked far into the countryside to a tiny, stone chapel, reaching it as the sun broke through the mist over the green-gray meadows. With Xavier I discovered the lady inside me—the gentleness and finesse I had not felt during my months as the activist. I loved every minute of it, but sensed that he and I would not survive together outside the rose garden we had so completely constructed. On some level I already knew, and was steeling myself against, the one truth we did not discuss–that I, or any woman, could not be the love he was searching for.

That fall I extended my time away from the sober intensity of Smith by studying at Bowdoin for a year. In the co-ed smaller college, not far from the sea in my mother's Maine, I felt relaxed and immediately drawn into the community of actors and artists. I started photographing again and signed on for the role of Mother in *Ah, Wilderness!*—a slight but fun romp by Eugene O'Neill. One night, while still in my fine lady mood from Oxford, I was sitting in state in the apartment of Tim, one of my close actor friends, as a party warmed up. In walked a tall, lanky guy with long blond hair, whose quietness stood out from the raucous fun of the line dance forming to do the "bump" to the Pointer Sisters. Jan and I ended up talking and then continued the conversation over dinners, discovering our shared interests in intentional communities, music, and art. I watched him play guitar with his band in a bar downtown and he listened to my rehearsals for the play. I enjoyed the fun and camaraderie of the cast, but tried to ignore the anxiety of memorizing my lines and the fact that opening night was scheduled on the anniversary of Geoff's death. Days before the performance I broke out in hives and I knew this was becoming tougher than I let on. When I finally stood with the cast in the lights of the curtain call, trussed up in my corset and Victorian dress, my hair pulled up in a dignified twist, I took my first full breath all evening, relieved that I had spurned my ghost.

The following week I headed home for Thanksgiving break, ready to share new photographs and tales of the play with my parents and Daphne. They greeted me with uncharacteristic seriousness. At the kitchen table my father finally explained, his eyes tired and sad. "Bethy. Rick's plane crashed." My mind flashed an image of Rick, a smashed plane, the jungle of Vietnam—as if on television news. "They haven't found the plane yet," my father said, his voice tight. "So right now he's 'missing.'"

"Missing." Not there, lost, gone—Maz in his red baseball cap and that grin. A tidal wave of emotion picked me up and took me to my father. I wrapped my arms around him, and we stood there, his big body hugging back, holding on, Daphne and Mom sitting at the table, each of us crying, feeling, "Here we go again. Here we go." And the terrifying hole of blackness and grief just reached up and swallowed us whole, once again.

In the next leaden days, we finally began to hear more. Rick had escorted two girls who were paraplegics to a home in Saigon where they would live and receive special care. A monsoon set in and he was stranded in the city, making busy work for himself for several days. Finally, on Saturday, November 17, two pilots decided to brave the trip north to Quang Ngai. One turned back soon after getting up in the air because the turbulence was too threatening. Rick's pilot on Air Vietnam kept going. A little while later, lost in the fog and the slashing rain, the plane crashed blindly into the side of a mountain.

At Quang Ngai, the leaders of the Quaker team organized a search party to find the wreckage. It was difficult because the crash was high in the mountains and in disputed territory, so searchers were at risk just getting to the site. But finally, after calls between the Quakers, the State Department, and the South Vietnamese military, a band of soldiers and local people who knew Rick found the crushed plane in a deep recess of cliffs and trees. The day before Thanksgiving, Rick was identified, his six-foot-long body surrounded by small ones. In his wallet, they found a school photo of Geoff, age eleven, smiling quietly. Only later did we realize that November 17, the day Rick had

Our cousin Rick
and the photo of
Geoff he kept in
his wallet.

been killed, was November 16 in American Eastern Standard Time, the eighth anniversary of my brother's suicide.

Rick's massive coffin—built without a single nail by the Vietnamese carpenters with whom he had worked—was filled with forty pounds of tea leaves. Following Eastern tradition, his body was carefully cleaned and wrapped in muslin by his Vietnamese and American friends. They honored him and his family in traditional Vietnamese custom, then lowered him into the coffin and burned it on a funeral pyre, collecting his ashes to be flown home and buried at Abington Friends Meeting House in Pennsylvania. Rick's family and friends, and all our cousins, gathered for a memorial service, once again silenced into disbelief and sorrow. Then, in the gray November chill we walked out to Rick's grave—right next to Geoff's under the huge old tree. On one side its branches looked down on my Quaker Minister Grandfather Taylor and family members. On the other side of the tree, the two simple headstones of his only grandsons: Geoffrey Rowell Taylor, 1951–1965, and Richard Warren Thompson, 1949–1973. Numbly, I stared at the two white stones on the gray, dark earth. There was no peace here. They were just so very gone. And with them, this war. For me, their deaths—in 1965 and 1973—began and ended the Vietnam War.

When I returned to Bowdoin, I retreated into the solitude of Jan's off-campus room. I told him about Rick, more about our family, Geoff. He slept beside me each night, understanding my need to be just held. I missed the whirl of my theater group, but I needed his quiet comfort as I felt blindly through the tunnel of deep sadness for Rick. One evening, after a day of feeling particularly fine together, Jan and I lay down and as he reached for me, knowing what he wanted, I found myself finally confessing I had never truly slept with anyone before and I was scared. He was quiet for a bit, and then chuckled, said, "Well, I hadn't expected THAT." I felt horrendous, tried to say something about my Victorian upbringing and being screwed up by trauma. He didn't press the issue. But as the days went on, I only felt uglier, more fucked-up, and all the more unable to relax with him. I was asking a lot of his patience, and inevitably it ended.

For three days I stayed in my room, tortured by the feeling that I could not love, and that I had just lost the one person who could have helped me try. I felt trapped. Guys seemed drawn to my energy, and then moved by my vulnerability. But that same sadness held them at a distance, locked out by my sober penitence, my obeisance to sorrow. Grief for Geoff, now Rick, seemed to fill my heart, leave no room. So lovers moved on, to someone more able to play. As Jan said, I needed to loosen up more, "go with the flow." But I couldn't.

I threw myself into studying and then acting again, this time a one-act written by a student based on a story he had heard in Ireland. I was Mary, a young woman whose mother had just been killed in a freak car accident and whose husband was a drunk, unable to bring in his share of the crops. He hated their baby girl, just two weeks old, because she was not a boy who could help on the farm. In despair, Mary wondered should she kill her own child? Inside her mind and heart, I had to go through thirty minutes of excruciating weeping, low pensiveness, delirium, and fond memories–and I loved it, lived it for weeks. In each performance I felt purged, emptied out, venting extreme versions of every emotion I felt in my own life, but in a socially acceptable play. One night, a drunken young man at a fraternity party declared he had fallen in love with me on that stage. We sat on the porch steps in the spring night, confessing hopes and fears to each other in a sodden soul embrace. Then we stumbled back to my room where we made sloppy, not too good love to each other before passing out. Joe and I only saw each other occasionally after that, but we felt protective of each other, and I felt relieved to know I was not totally bereft of trust and desire—and the ability to act upon it.

That summer of 1974, still feeling the presence of Rick, I decided it was time to try my own hand at Quaker service. So, with Watergate unfolding in the background, I followed my mother's example and helped lead a Quaker work camp of high school volunteers in the mountains of Kanawha County of West Virginia. As the national oil crisis plunged the poor into heating emergencies, we insulated the shacks of families hidden deep in the forests and hollows of the ancient southern Appalachian Mountains. To buffer the winter's cold, we nailed aluminum flashing around the bottoms of dried-out wood frames that sat up on brick piles, and we laid insulation into attics. I fell in love with the beauty of the mountains–driving our packed VW bus through steep, curving roads that wound from breath-taking vista to craggy cliffs to huddled towns—even as I was shaken by the depth of poverty. Flies settled on food in dishes left unwashed on greasy counters. Newspapers, tacked up against wood slat walls, barely kept the wind out. One child did the shopping when the welfare check came because her mother couldn't read. In 104-degree heat, I dressed in long sleeves and pants and climbed up into crawl-space attics to lay prickly fiberglass insulation, my body pouring sweat, the hard physical labor a satisfying penance.

With the families' permission, I photographed them and took down their oral histories, which would become part of my honors thesis in American Studies. I had pored over James Agee's *Let Us Now Praise Famous Men*, and although at times I too romanticized these people's grit, I understood that not every person saw our help as a gift. One elderly woman shooed us away, said, "Don't you turn my house into a pigsty!" But most families pitched in to bang nails or cut flashing with our team. Mrs. Huffington sat on her porch in a deep, green valley, and swept her hand up toward the mountain beyond. "No one's here to take over for me, dear. Why don't you come on down. Buy the farm. Whole thing–house, barn, fields, equipment–kind of old, but with a little work, OK—$11,000. What say?" I was touched, and wished I were in a place in my life to take her up on it. But already, as I studied the world through literature and photographs, I knew my old dream of being a farmer's wife was fading. This farm would be someone else's new start.

It was around this time that a cousin of my father's—a cousin who loved my father dearly—said to Daphne, "You know, in a way, there's a blessing in Geoffy's death. It gave your father a chance to finally see you two wonderful girls." Daphne and I were both beginning to feel our talents were being valued by the outside world as well as by our parents, and we were off, trying to let go of the long, heavy arm of our family's grief. For Daphne the release came when she headed north to the Rhode Island School of Design. When I visited her, I saw quickly she was working hard at finding her way in its bohemian world of black leather and oil paint, studio work until midnight and rooms full

Visiting with Mrs. Huffington.

of constantly creating people—required to sketch in their little black books anywhere they sat down. She was producing more art than ever before, and feeling estranged from our family's ways as she started to define what an artist's life might be.

As Daphne and I reunited away from the home where our sadness lay, more and more we just goofed together and fell into a deep, easy connection. Once, she came up to Smith and we headed to a fraternity at Amherst, took over the dance floor, jitterbugging to exhaustion. We knew we were a bit odd for preferring each other as dance partners. We looked enough alike that people thought we were twins; but with her colorful, homespun skirt and peasant blouse, her striking eyes and high cheekbones, she was the head-turner, and I was proud and happy to be with her. When November 16 came my senior year, I grabbed my friend Maria, jumped in another friend's car, got to Daphne's studio in Providence by nine at night, took her out for wine, hugs, and girl-talk in a candle-lit bar until the awful moments after ten o'clock were passed, and then got back on the road to be at Smith for morning classes. We were not heavy partiers or cavalier students, but when that hole in our lives occasionally sliced through the busyness of our days, it helped to drop our temporal duties and find each other to just feel the comfort of the only other person in the world who knew without speaking the ache of our particular past.

In the spring of 1975, during my last months of college, I was reading the reports of the pull-out from Vietnam and wrestling with the feeling that my logical, fated next step was to follow Rick, work in Vietnam with the Quakers, help the transition to peace. I gave Linda, Rick's girlfriend, a call. She greeted me like a big sister, and we talked a long time. She remembered our house—its "warmth and casual, earthy elegance," eating Philadelphia fried scrapple at the round kitchen table as my mother bustled around them. She remembered Rick and my father laughing uproariously over a favorite New Yorker cartoon. And finally, she remembered visiting my parents after Rick's death, and my father taking her to Abington Meeting House. "Your father and I spent a long, quiet visit there, lying under the trees and remembering a very special young man." I told her of my feeling of fate—that I should go to Quang Ngai. Again like a big sister, she said firmly, "Your family has lost enough. You don't have to do this."

So I went off to teach at Moses Brown, a Quaker boys school just about to go co-ed in Providence, Rhode Island, not far from Daphne. Some of my students were boys the age my brother had been when he died. I was excited to teach them literature, but I also hoped I took with me a fine-tuned antenna that might feel when they were struggling, in need of a reassuring word.

Unpeaceable Kingdom

Providence in 1975 was a dying city, its downtown dark and windy. But up on the hill, I felt a biblical sense of destiny. I settled into my first classroom and began to enjoy the freedom of a paycheck and my own apartment, car, and schedule. I felt optimistic, confident that my life was on track, that I was ready to become the teacher and independent adult I had imagined. For the first time in years, I felt freed from my past, ready to start fresh, ready for some fun in life. Enough of sorrow! I thought.

Soon, I was smitten with Jim, who taught biology at the school. A kind, midwestern man, with an easy sense of humor, he had left Iowa for the Peace Corps during Vietnam, even as his brother-in-law went off to the war. Jim's return had been much like many a Vietnam veteran: nobody knew what to say, or even to ask. He was so changed in his view of the world that he could not bear to stay in the orderly Lutheran life of his forebears. So he came east searching for a more sympathetic culture. He found it at Moses Brown, just before I showed up to teach English for a few years.

Within Jim's embrace I felt whole and happy for the first time since childhood. We fit well, and I was calmed by his quieter nature. We left notes in each other's school mailboxes, grabbed hands for a quick walk between classes, sped home for love lunches. For a heady year I just sailed on top of the world, and felt ten years younger. As a friend said, "When you showed up at this school, you were eighty years old. Now, you're going on sixteen." Maybe, I thought, I was finally going to do some catch-up, enjoy some of the casual fun that eluded me in my teens.

But in my second year of teaching, as November got closer, I felt the insidious tendrils of sadness and anxiety begin to suck the confidence out of me once again. I tried to shake it off. I mean, here I was, passionately in love with someone who seemed to really love me too. But, even as I was thrilling to every time alone with Jim, deep inside I just wanted to lie down and cry for a long, long time. I wanted him to somehow crawl inside there with me and hold my heart so it would stop hurting; I wanted him to fill that chasm of grief forever. I thought such love would heal me. But it wasn't happening. I began to think that maybe it was time, with the comfort of Jim's care, to go into some kind of therapy. I was scared because nobody I knew did that—therapy was for sick people, less-than-functioning people. Publicly, I was of the brave, stiff upper lip, productive leader tradition; to strangers, you didn't open yourself to even the appearance of vulnerability—such wavering could imply moral weakness. But how could I be sad and anxious when I was feeling such love in my life? I went to the counselor who consulted for our school. I had met her once when one of my students was writing about suicide and I wanted to know how to respond as a teacher. Now I went for myself.

It was in these sessions, as I stripped away the layers of sadness, that I began to say out loud views I had not had words for before. That Geoff was maybe not just a martyr to the war. That my father, the voice of Quaker history—a history of tolerance and equality— was actually sometimes intolerant and wounding to the women in his family. Had he been like that to Geoff? That my mother, who I still saw as the perfect complement for my feisty nature, and who I knew had always been a sympathetic ear for Geoff, might also have been a suppressing influence on him, showing him he must turn the other cheek, just as she always did with my father.

When I began to see the darker side of my family's dynamics, my visits home became painful, particularly with my father, who brought up memories of Geoff constantly, and who dominated table conversations with diatribes and anecdotes from his own life, all of which we had heard before. Daphne, Mom, and I, sometimes Jim, all learned to nod and get through it as politely as possible. But there were times I just got up from the table and left what I now thought of as the "Death-house."

One thing I learned in my readings at the time was that there are often parallels between the family of a suicide and the family of an alcoholic. Both a suicide and an alcoholic control the other family members' behavior by the violence—emotional or physical—of their own actions. Like a drunk, Geoff's choice still held punishing sway over our anxieties; like a drunk, my father controlled any room he was in—although because he didn't drink much, he would be called a "dry drunk." Tough love said, both a drunk and a suicide must be "let go," separated from one's self so the survivor can move on. The drinking and the suicide must be seen as crimes you had nothing to do with, the way you might feel if your sibling robbed a store because they had a drug problem. Tough love said it's their problem, not yours–separate your heart, your sense of responsibility. But, oh, I was finding that hard to do.

Most painful was watching my mother as she began to show signs of strain. She never smoked or drank; she also didn't exercise much–even though she had once climbed mountains, bicycled cross-country, and skied New England slopes. As a mom, she just paid close attention to taking care of the family, without complaint. Whatever sadness and stress she felt got buried in her body. She was still a wonderful hug to come home to, but around this time, as Daphne and I visited less frequently, she seemed more and more anxious. She fretted about Jim and me choosing to live together, and wondered how serious we were.

One morning during a summer visit, after Jim and Dad had left the kitchen, I started to clear the table. Mom stayed seated. "Do you understand that marriage is being able to pull together as a team no matter what?" she asked.

"Yes," I said carefully. "But we want to let each other become whatever each needs to become. Our motto is to be 'alone together.'"

"He's much older than thee. Have you had a blood test to make sure you can both have babies?" she asked.

"Mom! We're in LOVE! We're not talking blood tests!" I dismissed her pragmatism as perverse.

She was quiet for a bit and I gathered bowls by the sink. "Thee says thee's in love, but thee seems skittish and down."

"Oh, Mom. I've got a lot on my mind–nothing to do with Jim. I just find it hard to talk about some things with thee and Dad. You guys always seem so certain all the time. You never seem down—"

She looked right at me. "What do you think, Beth? That sixty-year-old people don't get depressed?"

And then it was clear. I had always thought of her as rightfully sad after Geoff's death. But I had never thought of her as seriously depressed. She had always kept busy, tending to my father, the house, our family gatherings. She still helped out in Bryn Gweled functions and managed "The Friendly Crafters" to raise money for Quaker activities. But now I saw the wide, gray expanse of her loneliness ripple out before me, and I heard her say "you" with impatience and disdain. "What do you think, Beth?" So, sixty-year-old people get depressed. In my self-involved twenties I assumed it was only we the struggling, searching, pre-marrieds who suffered.

I did finally tell my parents I was in therapy trying to figure out some of the "control issues" in our family. My parents expressed support as if I were the only one in the family that had this problem of seeing our family as troubled. Only later would I understand, through R. D. Laing's *Politics of the Family,* that often, when one member of the family tries to uncover the family's hurtful patterns, the rest of the family comforts itself by designating the "messenger" as "sick." They are thus relieved of responsibility in the family pain, and can transfer their self-doubts onto the one they deem unwell.

Before we left, my mother took Jim aside and said, "Now be careful, don't hurt her, she's been through a lot, and we don't want any more tragedies in her life."

She meant well, but of course I resented her meddling. And of course it didn't help. Despite my mother's anxious plea to Jim, in another year he decided to leave me. He was tired, I think, of my incessant self-analysis, my general anxiety about how we were doing, and what should we work on now to make the relationship better. Partly we were under the sway of the times—of consciousness "raising" and self-"actualizing" in every part of life—work, love, sex, and creative outlets. But mostly I know now it was still Geoff, lurking like an unsettled ghost, unresolved in his sadness, and penetrating my ostensibly successful adult life with undying pleas for attention. In the comfort of feeling so loved for the first time in my life, I had finally let the floodgates open, and the torrent of memory and understanding was finally too much for my lover to bear.

One night, I dragged Jim out of a party to discuss some revelation about my father; another night I ran out of gas in a dangerous neighborhood because I was so distracted I forgot to stop at the gas station. At night, after schoolwork, I loosened my heart over wine and spewed words into my journal–a rush of scenes, comments, and feelings that left me calm, emptied, and, I see now, locked in my own fascinating world. I think Jim realized intuitively that part of me would always be lost to my past, and that I wanted him to save me. But he knew he couldn't, that no one could. One day as I washed dishes silently beside him, he said, "I can't reach you, Lizzy. You go into these depressions and there's nothing I can do or say to help. You're just far away." A few months later he said, "I still love you, but these days I don't like you." This was why, he said, we needed to "split."

I didn't understand. I thought this was all just part of a relationship. Why did it have to end? I remembered friends had asked, grinning, "So, do you guys fight yet?" and I had thought, "Good heavens, is that the key to a healthy relationship?" Jim and I had never fought over anything. But now, as everything good seemed to be slipping from my grasp, I wondered, should I challenge his dictum that we must "split"? Finally, feeling strangled, I tried to tell him how much I loved him. One night when he went off to see an old friend, I left a note waiting for him on the counter in the kitchen. Drunkenly I scrawled in bright red crayon, "Fuck you, I love you; what are you afraid of?" I lay awake upstairs, waiting for him to come home, waiting for his response in the kitchen below. And then suddenly I was scared I would anger him. I had written "Fuck you." I hadn't said that out loud to anyone since I said it to Geoff the day he died. I couldn't do it. I crept downstairs and threw away the note. There would be no confrontation, no conflict, no unmanageable emotions. Like my mother, I squashed the feelings, no matter how intense, and willed myself to turn the other cheek, accept the judgment of my man. But the trauma of losing the love I thought I would hold my whole life finally hurt worse than any of the deaths that came before. He went off to find his dream in the woods of Vermont, and I stayed behind, stupefied by confusion and grief once again.

A month after we parted, on a hot July day in 1978, I was alone in the darkroom of an old factory space I shared with fellow photographers. There in the womblike darkness of the developing room, as I felt through the steps of loading my film onto the tank reel I could not see, my fingers worked mechanically while my heart and mind wrapped around Jim and my love for him, and now my loss of him. I felt so fucked up and wrong, so alone and lost. And suddenly my mind segued to Geoff, a young lean teenager just gazing at me like in the last photograph I ever took of him—standing behind our wheelbarrow with a Halloween pumpkin resting on the wide metal wheel and our old collie dog sitting on his haunches beside him. The sky was October blue, the vines were green, his flannel shirt was red, and his jeans blue and dirty. He was holding the dog's collar, and looking at the camera, showing no particular emotion, just doing what he was told as I took his birthday picture for posterity, just three weeks before he would

The last photo taken of Geoff.

decide he too just didn't want to be there . . . And suddenly that connection was clear—first Geoff, now Jim, just wrenching themselves
away when they couldn't take it anymore, checking out without a by-
your-leave, walking away, just leaving me there with my pain, leaving,
leaving . . . gone . . .

In the blackness of that darkroom, I gripped the metal developing
tank harder and harder as some kind of knot inside me tightened and
tightened, and then a swift surge of pain threw itself up through my
body, out through my lungs and arms, and suddenly I was screaming
and throwing that tank, and grabbing whatever metal, glass, and wood
I could get my hands on—smashing, against the wall, against the floor,
smashing against the sink, none of which I could see, but all of which
I knew exactly what it was and where it was and what I had just done
to it.

Probably it was over in a few minutes. But what had left me felt like
thirteen years of rage. Geoff really was no longer the good martyr. He
was no longer the victim. I was. He didn't have to live with the legacy
of his suicide. I did. And now Jim's giving up on me made it all clear
and fresh again. It was not OK. And if these boys I loved were going to
have the last say, they wouldn't have it without me finally screaming
to the skies that their decisions stank, and they were wrong, wrong,
wrong themselves. No longer was I going to take the rap. No longer
was I going to play the second-best sister, the also-ran lover, the sick
daughter . . .

A friend found me standing still, silenced, in the middle of the
white-walled studio. He looked in at the darkroom, and then suggested I go back into therapy. I went dutifully one more time, to hear
a kind man say, "This all sounds very appropriate." But I knew from
then on, I could figure out whatever I needed to figure out on my own.
Actually, I was proud of the violence of my rage. I mean, the real question was, why had it taken me so long to be this angry? Something
in me had snapped, had truly let go, and I felt strangely emptied out,
lighter, maybe even ready to embrace, on my own terms–not Jim's, or
my parents', or Geoff's terms—whatever came at me. But what were
my own terms?

I decided to leave the familiar script of Quaker education and I
started to pick up work as a feature writer and photographer. At night

I wrote for myself—journals and short stories about a young woman trying to understand moments of revelation about human connection and essential loneliness. The responses were startling. At one public reading, when I described a character who killed himself out of the blue, some listeners started laughing. I went to an older writer for advice, and he said, well, it sounds kind of like a Faulkner novel—all tragic but grimly funny, and, by the way, do you want to spend the night? A friend came with a theater director's proposal—turn my journals into a play; my friend said, "turn it into a musical!—with your father up there as a judge in long flowing robes, the witnesses singing their tragicomic pleas for understanding, and a kind of Greek chorus over to the side singing comments about religious hubris and male animus off and on." And then at a conference a famous writer read my stories, and he said, very calmly, "You say you're a pacifist, but you carry a gun." Bam!

At the age of twenty-six, in a kind of volcanic eruption of my sense of myself, I realized I had been following a rather simplistic set of rules: work hard, be a good daughter and Quaker, and the good life is yours. Talk the talk, and you will walk the walk. But clearly I was not. My family didn't fit anymore. I had blown it with the love of my life. I was not calm and kind and gentle. No, I was passionate, earnest, stern, and furious. Furious at the sadness and anxiety that seemed to mark my life, erode my relationships. Furious that in death my brother had become a kind of godhead in whose shadow no mortal, particularly a sister in a family that revered sons, could measure up. No wonder, at the newspaper where I worked during that glowering time, a reporter told my editor I was "intimidating."

For a year or two I swam in the big dark pit, a defiant loner who drank too much. During the day, I pulled myself carefully out of hangovers to write features for the Sunday newspaper, shoot photo jobs, or teach as a writer-in-residence in schools around Rhode Island. At night I drank and wrote and read, grateful that I had the busyness of interviewing, teaching, or darkroom work the next day to keep me moving. I was poor, never presuming to ask my parents for help as I survived on freelance or arts council checks that came fitfully and far apart. I lived alone in a poor neighborhood, ate hot dogs and macaroni, learned to tune and oil my VW bug by myself, shopped for clothes

at the Salvation Army, dragged back an armchair abandoned on tl
sidewalk. Like Tennessee Williams, I thought, my life is now depen-
dent on the kindness of strangers. Sometimes in my loneliness, my
ghosts would float up through the preoccupations of my life in unex-
pected moments—Jim's walk, Geoff's giggle, Rick's grin, Tony's beard.
Or a man would look like what I thought one of them would look like
now, and I would think, "What a . . ." And words would fail me.

I pulled encouragement from anywhere I could find it. I read that
Katharine Hepburn had discovered her brother after he killed himself
when they were teenagers, and I decided she was my soul mentor; if
she survived that, and was as cool and competent as she was, then I
could be too. I discovered Bonnie Raitt was raised a good Quaker girl
and had plunged into alcohol abuse. OK, I thought, there it is again—
we're raised to be so good and pure, but we get out in the real world
and bam, we blow out all the stops as soon as we get the chance! I read
Doris Lessing's *Golden Notebook* and started to play with different
voices in my own journals, my different selves—Earth Mother Essie,
Dizzy Lizzy, and Limping Lou-Lou. I read Anaïs Nin's confessionals,
and pushed myself to write more boldly about sex and taboos. For
the most part, though, I railed in my journals about the tragedies of
life and always ended with some version of a determined howl that, as
disco diva Gloria Gaynor was declaring all over the radio then, I would
survive.

At least one friend was not so sure. She had seen me weep as I
scraped off old wallpaper and painted her house. After hours of sand-
ing floors together, she watched as I sloshed away my senses in vodka
and tonics. She had seen my recent photographic self-portrait: starkly
black and white, my pale, naked back to the camera, curled on the
floor in a corner of one of those stripped, empty rooms, the great rips
of wallpaper tossed like chaotic waves around me—alone, isolated,
vulnerable. One day a few months later I answered the phone to hear
her surprised voice. "Oh! You're home Beth! I've been trying for three
days to get you! I was beginning to worry–I'm sorry—I just thought–
you've been so down–that maybe, when I couldn't reach you–oh I don't
know, I thought maybe you'd reached a point–you know—like your
brother . . ." I was amazed. It hadn't dawned on me that suicide would
ever be an option for myself. Particularly now that I had discovered

my rage at Geoff's choice, the idea of giving up as he had hadn't even entered my imagination. But I was grateful for her care. "You feel like a guardian angel, Pen. I didn't even know you were there."

I settled into what seemed like the comforts of my drink-defined life. What the hell, I thought–everybody does it; I'm functioning fine; it feels good. But over a hung-over coffee one morning, my writer-friend Lissa asked carefully, did I think I had a drinking problem? I was startled into silence and fear. Again, I felt floored that someone cared enough to be so bold with me. And I worried: was I really so weak that I had this sordid problem? I found a book on women and alcoholism and saw how neatly I fit the profile: If men found a favorite bar and validated their problem in the company of men, women–I— kept it secret. I drank alone, threw away bottles in varied trash cans, only bought enough at one time to make the stash look moderate, bought at varied liquor stores so I didn't feel like a "regular." I hadn't even realized I had become so cagey; I had just dismissed it as a bad time in my life and I deserved to let it all go for a bit. In fact, I kind of liked being a bad girl–whizzing down the highway in my yellow VW bug "Banana" after a day photographing a wedding, the radio on full blast, a half-pint of whiskey in my driving hand.

Most friends couldn't see, and I maintained professional competence just enough so employers didn't suspect. Daphne saw. And in her usual way, like my mother, she said nothing openly. But one day on a train together, as we sat soaking up the sunlight that poured in upon us, she reached over and brushed the hair out of my eyes, a touch she had never offered before, a caretaking that my body immediately, instinctively rose to, as if remembering a kind of intimacy it had forgotten it needed. I closed my eyes and she held her hand on my cheek a moment more, letting me know she was there.

One day in May, I woke up hung over and disgusted with myself. I was tired. Tired of being sick. Tired of putting out so much energy to hide the consuming and sobering up, again and again and again. Off and on I had wanted to stop. Now I was determined. In my haze that day I threw away the bottles, put the AA books on the shelf, and wondered how I would do this. Suddenly I heard my earth mother self: Just visualize: remember when you were healthy, in high school, a fit and lean field hockey player; you didn't need wine then, you can be like that again now; just go back to the habits of when you were healthy. It felt like a revelation: Just visualize and BE what you once were!

The next day I taped colorfully drawn dictums to my wall. One ordered me to "WriteRunWriteRunWriteRunWriteRun . . ." over dozens of lines. Another quoted the AA acronym "HALT: Never get too Hungry, Angry, Lonely, or Tired." I considered going to an AA meeting, but what would I learn? My brotherly friend Nick had given me his books from AA; I had read them all; I got the point. I particularly liked how, as Nick said, the AA system seemed Quakerly: it believed that truth, healing, knowledge came from the self and one's relationship with a personal sense of God, the spirit. "Let go, let God," said the AA adage. Let God take over, take care, call the shots. I could hear that healing spirit in me—what I had once called the Inner Light, but which now felt more humanized—calling, reassuring, reminding me it had not left me. What AA offered, and I didn't have right then, was company. It was time to come out of my cave.

With Lissa, I helped start a "journal collective"–women reading from their journals in public performances, which, to our surprise and pleasure, quickly gained a following. I read old excerpts—about the "lovely mess" of my life and mind as ex-lover, struggling writer, boozing loner defending myself against a cacophony of condemning voices in my head; about an Autumn day, when, as I walked off my hangover, I suddenly felt Geoff gazing down at me quietly through the clouds, studying the back of my shorn head—and I realized it was November 16, my brother had become God, and that was not good; and about a week when lovers from past lives came back to back and pulled me from my loneliness to teach me that maybe, sometimes, it was OK to let the body have a good time.

Soon, Lissa and our friend Nancy said, let's get a place together. In a funky apartment in Fox Point, the Portuguese neighborhood of Providence, we set about to create our own sense of home, complete with a big, shaggy dog named Samovar. Dubbed "the Three Graces" by a friend, we carried each other through a complicated period of transition. Over vegetable wok concoctions we talked long into weekend nights–about our trials with men, our comforts with women, different kinds of love, writers who moved us, the families we came from, the siblings who saved us, the teachers who showed us who we wanted to be, the anxieties that woke us in the middle of the night, the philosophies that offered some solace. Always, we laughed a lot and enjoyed a frank, easy camaraderie. Slowly, with their help, I began to regain some confidence. I realized I had changed: I felt chastened, less passionate, but somehow more realistic. On some deep primal level I was just glad to be alive. And differences about how to be alive—as a good Quaker, or a good feminist, or a good liberal, all those moral "shoulds" I had assumed—just didn't seem so important anymore.

As I began to see how each of us struggled with our pasts, with the limits of relationships and of our own personalities, I realized I wasn't alone in feeling my love-life and family were flawed. More important, I saw this WAS life–everybody's life. Most lives were defined by some set of ideals that inevitably crashed hard against the real compromises of life. Many people struggled with the poisoning effects of loss and anger, until they realized the poison was killing them, and if they were to survive, they needed to let it go, find some acceptance in whatever way they could.

What did I need to let go? What accept? Slowly, I began to realize I needed to forgive my good Quaker family for setting me up with such hard-to-please goals. Or at least I had to forgive myself for not attaining my version of those goals—the perfect, unconflicted, angerless, politically correct, good Quaker life. There was no way around the facts: I was never going to live the homemade, Quaker Meeting, kind and gentle, lefty liberal life I had been raised in. I had loved it, but it had blown up the night Geoff died. The memories were nice to visit. But the adult I had become no longer fit. My rage and alcoholism, my disillusions and failures had blown open the idyll, shown it to have been a cocoon from which I had to extricate myself if I were to adjust to the complexities of my life. My lingering pain was no longer the fault of anybody or any group; it was just a part of me–my wound to accept and heal as best I could. I refused the alternative–to be handicapped. It was time to let go and try for something new.

Daphne and me in 1978 and 1979.

Family

Bill Collins was a tough, "hard" news reporter at the *Providence Journal* where I was writing "soft" features on subjects like disco queens, women in rock and roll, alternative schools, and radical Rhode Islanders. On Memorial Day in 1979, he put his wife on the train as she left him for good to find her dream in New York City, and he went home to pick up the Sunday newspaper. He found an article of mine that followed Adrian Hall, our local theater director, down to his Texas roots, through his bold and raunchy creative evolution, to his fame as the soul of Trinity Square Repertory Company. Bill liked my writing, and a year later, when my editor told him she thought we should meet, he pulled himself out of his post-divorce depression to walk by my computer station. Seeing a Margaret Atwood novel lying on my desk, he groused dryly, "No Kierkegaard in the newsroom!" He gave me a sideways glance, and walked on.

At a party soon after, we proceeded to argue—about theater, the sixties, Vietnam, feminism, religion, the atom bomb, and children. He was my counter-ego; he saw most things almost exactly the opposite from me. But a few weeks later, on an official date, he told me about reading my article and we began to find common ground in our loves of writing, movies, and music. At work, in that pre-email era, he started leaving me computer files of love-song lyrics. From an old Cole Porter song: "I've got you under my skin . . . I've got you deep in the heart of me . . ." From *Gigi:* "You—do—something to me, something that simply mystifi-I-I-es me. Tell me, tell me it's true . . . Do that voodoo that you do so well . . ." Nobody in my folky group of friends even knew these songs. Bill was a puzzle to me–infuriating and interesting at once; I had never met anyone like him. And, perhaps because I had begun to doubt the presumptions of my past, I decided to listen to him. In our spirited arguments, we were both intrigued; somehow we offered each other compelling information that helped us move away from the extremes we had held onto for comfort.

Then November came, the month that always ate away at me, no matter how well I was feeling about my life. Bill came for dinner by chance the night of the sixteenth. He knew about Geoff and how he had died, what we knew and didn't know. We lay down that night and I was withdrawn, turned away from him, swirling into the dread that washed over me on this night, every year.

"What's wrong?" he asked, circling his arm around me.

What could I say? I'm sad? It sounded so childlike, so something I should have gotten over long ago. And, really, hadn't I? All that therapy, and readjustments with my parents, and Jim's loss trumping the pain of Geoff forever? I couldn't think straight. I just wanted to be held, quietly. But life was never quiet with Bill. It was provocative and sexually charged. There was no space for moping. Together we did things, worked hard, debated intensely, pushed each other. But I couldn't let my sadness go. This was my day to mourn; he should let me grieve, be there for me. "This is the night Geoff died," I said.

He was quiet. Then he withdrew his arm from around me, lay back against the pillow, said slowly, "I want you to get this ghost of your brother out of our bed."

I lay there, frozen. He might as well have slapped me. What a cruel thing to say. I felt beaten. There was nothing I could say in return. He left soon after. Later in the night, staring into the darkness, my mind replayed his words over and over again. So cruel. Get the ghost of your brother out of our bed. Our bed. Geoff's a ghost. He's still here. In our bed. Have I made Geoff a lover? Yuk! But I have loved loving him, his ghost, for so long; he's so comfortably in me, with me. But haven't I kicked him out? After Jim? After sobering up? I don't think of him for days now. But, dear God, he's still here. My head reeled. I felt like Jason in Faulkner's *The Sound and the Fury*—in an ancient carriage rushing furiously around an old family monument, going nowhere, filled with helpless rage and determination. Get the ghost out of our bed. OUR bed. Bill and me. Get the ghost out of our bed. What a necessary step if I am truly going to move forward into new life. New life. That is what I want. What I want. And I will do whatever it takes to make it happen.

Bill and I moved in together and laid out our differences for clear airing. He believed that maybe it's a luxury to be a pacifist, that it's a stand that sometimes precludes being able to actually participate in government, so it lets most Quakers stand on the sidelines of difficult decisions. Its corollary, to be "in the world but not of it," sometimes inhibits one from participating in crucial parts of our democracy—in legislatures, boardrooms, and public school systems, for instance. And the comfort and beauty of life in Bryn Gweled, he reminded me, was counterbalanced by its requirement of membership. "How can BG stand for pluralism and equality when it employs a potentially exclusive membership process?" he asked. "It's really just another gated community." Bill learned from me that "soft" ways of seeing can be helpful. When he left journalism to become the think-tank for our mayor, Bill used words he had argued about with me—encouraging the mayor to be less pugilistic and to think in terms of "community" more. Even though Bill was impatient with theater and loved movies, he helped the mayor to save the repertory company I had written of in that article he liked. As we drove down Hope Street in Providence one day, he showed me the new storm windows on the public high school, and said he had helped find the money to put those in. It was then I realized that although we differed on many things, Bill actually made real good happen by getting into the dirt of government and finding the ways to put money where the mouths of activists sometimes stopped.

Intellectually, Bill and I shared a similar résumé. Raised in Boston, he had gone to Wesleyan and Harvard's Kennedy School of Government. Emotionally, we shared histories of loved ones leaving us, and of having functioned well professionally while we each plunged into alcohol abuse. Before we met, we had pulled ourselves up by the bootstraps and stabilized our lives. We sympathized with the wounded passion in each other, and we admired the other's will to survive and to work hard. I accepted our inevitability as more important than cloud-walking love. I understood he was not like the mothering men to whom I had been drawn for comfort; he was more like my father, aggressively learned, critical more than tolerant. But I was willing to cope with that because somehow I knew he would never leave me, never walk out. His code of honor was a throwback to some ancient ideal of loyalty and commitment that transcended daily angst. His certitude could jump-start the life I longed for, I thought. It helped when Nick, my big-brother friend, said, after I asked him his view of Bill, "The one thing I know is, he adores you."

The marriage Bill and I made has never been easy, but it has worked. On our best days I know that, like Hepburn and Tracy, we edit each other well, if provocatively. It was almost a relief to discover I COULD argue with him—he so obviously deserved a good rebuttal. Somehow I didn't feel cowed, or scared to rock the boat with him as I had felt with Jim, who seemed so unquestionably good. And, losing Jim had taught me that no lover could be my healer, the balm for my soul. Only I could take care of myself, save myself. So I saw Bill as separate, an equal force in my life, flawed like me, not a savior.

Still, learning how to fight constructively was a painful evolution. I felt ill equipped. Quakerism, or my understanding of it, had taught me that anger on any level was wrong, to be avoided. But I now believed such suppression may have undermined Geoff; certainly, my fear of conflict had not helped me hold on to Jim. Now, in marriage, I was determined NOT to be passive, as my mother seemed. I had rarely seen her talk back to my father, even when he clearly deserved it. Bill led the way: he was the first boyfriend who was willing to stand up to my father. Earlier boyfriends had taken long, exhausted naps when visiting my family home, or said, wearily, "Boy! You have a talky family!" or wavered as they faced my father's questions, offered ostensibly out of conversational interest but clearly with judgment hanging in the air–about their parents, education, job, plans. Bill unabashedly presented himself and his provocative views without fear of my father, and something deep within me knew I needed his help to let go, truly let go, of my father's power and Geoff's legacy in my life.

Bill decided to take my name Taylor as his own in private life. Some friends thought his becoming a Taylor showed a streak of feminism in him. My father was grateful there would now be heirs with the last name Taylor. But by nature Bill has never cared about anyone's assumptions or expectations. I had never understood why the woman had to give up her name when she married, and I presumed he would agree. I assumed our children would take his name, perhaps with Taylor as a middle name. No, he said, he didn't hold my philosophy that a name at birth was one's identity forever. But if I cared that much about keeping my name, he realized he didn't care that much about his own, so he would change his name for us all to be one family in name. The nurses at Women and Infants Hospital loved him for that. Family was everything, and Bill was a hero. He did actually keep his "bachelor name" in public life. Because he was already well known as a journalist, and then as the mayor's policy director, he remained Collins downtown.

One day in April of 1984, I heard for the first time the glump-glump-glump of our first child's heartbeat. I walked out of the doctor's office in a euphoric state, started driving, and turned on the radio to hear: "State police have surrounded City Hall after sources claimed evidence of alleged corruption may have been destroyed." I envisioned Bill in his office, puffing dismissively on his cigar. Here I was with a healthy baby on the way, and Bill was down there trying to create good government even as rumors flared. That juxtaposition–of our attempt to lead a stable, upstanding life in the midst of melodrama around the mayor—became a kind of motif in our marriage. No files were found to be destroyed that day at City Hall, but the mayor was kicked out of office that spring anyway on charges that he had attacked his ex-wife's lover.

For the next few months, as Bill looked for work and I grew bigger with our baby, we drove over every road in Rhode Island, discovering country nooks and beautiful fields, old churches and funky fishing ports that made us fall deeply in love with our craggy state. Bill became the editor of a business magazine for a while, and then happily returned to City Hall when the mayor was reelected a few years later, ready to implement the renaissance of Providence. Knowing that the mayor was always under intense scrutiny as they rebuilt the city, Bill doggedly maintained his rigid ethical code. If we needed a new sidewalk, we couldn't ask the city to do it like every other citizen; we paid for it ourselves just to avoid people thinking, "Oh, Collins got a new sidewalk—must have been a gift from the mayor." If friends asked for favors, Bill withdrew from the relationship. Although his Puritan morality sometimes seemed overweening to me, I understood that like my Grandfather Taylor, he was "incorruptible"–and that is why the mayor hired him and listened to him.

As cruel fate would have it, our first son was born on my brother's birthday. He was due five days earlier, on October 20. But something made him wait—biology? Greek destiny? Faulknerian humor? My hospital bag was ready and waiting. October 21 . . . 22 . . . 23. Still waiting.

My cousin Terrie called. After her brother Rick died in Vietnam, she proudly and with good reason named her son Richie after him. Now she asked brightly, "Does thee have a name?"

"Not really. We're thinking of several—Peter, Andrew, Robert . . ."

"Well I can think of a really obvious one," she declared.

I was startled. "Thee means Geoff? . . . I couldn't do that, Terrie."

"Why ever not?"

"I just . . . I just want him to be his own person."

I knew she meant well. Only after I hung up the phone did I realize how far away from the family's myth about Geoff I had walked. To many others he was still a heroic, persecuted victim whose legacy could only be good. Was I the only one who saw he had also committed the most violent act imaginable and disfigured our lives forever? I mean, his death had manipulated my life, my emotions, my ability to love. It hadn't even dawned on me to place the mantle of that kind of power onto a child of mine. But Terrie's innocent question brought my fear into focus, and it would not go away: would Geoff's legacy of suicide continue to permeate my life and the lives of my children?

Together, Bill and I worked hard at creating a home and life for our three boys. The baby years were tiring, particularly as I juggled graduate school and teaching, and Bill believed a father's role was primarily financial support. "I'll know better what to do when they're teenagers," he said—and indeed he would, confidently researching and supporting their varied educational and career evolutions. For now, he pitched in to cook the weekend meals and we hired Margaret, whose calm, elderly presence helped stabilize our household. I taped the words of the so-called serenity prayer by our phone in the kitchen: "God, grant me the serenity to accept the things I cannot change, courage to change the things I can, and wisdom to know the difference." Knowing the difference was the hard part. But working toward that understanding helped me weather the frustrations in my marriage and enjoy the pleasures of my boys.

Often, in the baby kisses, the comforting heft of a toddler's body against my hip, small arm slung casually across my neck, I would feel my mother's mothering pass through me–the contented, this-is-the-reason-for-all-living sense of knowing. Who she had been before my brother died was the best part of who I was—my more generous, creative self, the wiser, calmer me. As I played with my boys in the pool, twirled them in wavelike waltzes, I sang as my mother had with us years before. "I like to catch brass rings on the merry-go-round, the one that goes up and down . . ." I followed my boys into moments of unfettered play and they drew me back into the world that was simple, straightforward, where the word "suddenly" once again meant thrill, surprise, and fun. Peter was clown faces, rock-and-roll performances, Michael Jackson's moonwalk, all tied to Zena, the brown-eyed beauty

My husband Bill and our three sons.

from next door, the two of them attached at the hip. Sam was curly hair, scholarly glasses, and goofy grin, quick to take a hand or cuddle, join a race down the street or in the pool. Max watched the older brothers for three years without a word, just chomped on his pacifier, built Lego rockets, castles, and cars. He would come barreling at me, and leap up to be caught, wrapping his legs and arms around my torso, nestling his head against my shoulder. "Perfect fit," we'd murmur. Having children began to fill that deep black hole in my heart; they opened up love like I had never known. And it never left.

Peter was six when he noticed the pictures of Geoff on my parents' walls. He knew I had a brother. He knew Geoff had died. Now he said, "Is that your brother?"

"Yes."

"How did he die?"

And there it was. How could I look at my innocent six-year-old and in one breath teach him that some people actually kill themselves, and that indeed his own flesh and blood, the guy whose birthday he was born on—that nice-looking guy in the picture with the smile and the blue eyes, and the light blue shirt I had ironed, the dark tie, and the Caesar haircut—chose to kill himself? The next question would be "how?" The next explanation would be "by hanging himself on a rope right there in Grammy's basement." I felt sick. Geoff's one bad night was still here socking it to us, and now it was about to start socking it to my defenseless little son. I wanted to scream at Geoff. To Peter I said, "He choked."

"How?"

Now I wanted to punch Geoff. "Somehow on a rope."

"How would he do that?"

I did not know how to lie like this. I felt dizzy. "We don't know really. It was an accident."

"Oh."

Thank God for the limits of a six-year-old mind. The word "accident" was familiar. We didn't have to go any further, at least not now.

Peter followed his friends into Boy Scouts and I held my tongue. The leader was a kind man I already knew and many of the families were from college hill where we lived. So maybe it was time for a new incarnation of the scouts. As a seven-year-old, Peter liked the smartness of the dress uniform, crafting a leather belt, hiking in Rhode Island hills, and traveling to Boston to see the Red Sox play.

One night, as I dropped him off at a scout meeting, I said hi to a mother of three boys who helped out as a den mother off and on.

"You let Peter do that?" She pointed at his earring in one ear and his short, braided ponytail curling down beneath his buzz-cut, a lightning bolt etched on each side of his shorn hair. This was the era of M.C. Hammer and the Backstreet Boys after all, and even at seven, Peter enjoyed a sense of setting his own style.

"Sure," I said warily. "What's the harm?"

"If my boy came home like that, I'd smack him," she said proudly.

This was a Boy Scouts I had hoped I wouldn't see. And perhaps it was just her; she was an extreme. Not long after, Peter came home from playing in a backyard with her boys and their pals, declaring them all to be jerks and out-of-control kids not worth his time. I gathered there had been a fight of some sort but Peter refused to give specifics. I pressed him and he mumbled something about super-soaker squirt guns, all of them ganged up, forcing him to drag them in a wagon, shooting at him. He stood there dripping, a towel draped damply around his neck. I pressed him further, trying to figure out if maybe he had done something to provoke them, wanting to be fair.

"No!"

He started to tear up, and the furies rose up in me for him.

"You know what you do with jerks like that, Pete?"

I gently took the towel from around his neck. Sam came in to the room, curious. I remembered Geoff's careful directions like it was yesterday. Neatly, I folded the towel into a triangle, then rolled it up into a long rat's tail.

"You whip 'em right back!" I snapped the towel into the air, cracking my hurt and rage for Peter into the invisible hip or butt of that scrawny bully with the mother who would "smack" a kid with an earring.

Peter stared at me.

"Cool!" said Sam.

Peter stayed with the scouts for a few years. At nine, he anxiously competed in the pinewood derby contest, piecing together and painting his model car, then racing it amidst the frenetic excitement of dozens of boys packed into a church basement. At eleven, he took a boom box and strobe light to help turn the basement into a haunted house that thrilled the neighborhood kids. Only years later did he describe how, for some scout meetings, there were no grown-ups, just older teenagers left in charge to practice leadership, and how some of them would let the older boys "pretend-fight" the younger boys to the point of bruising. "You were supposed to think it was fun, to just go along with it," Peter said. He shrugged off my concern. "The adults never knew; no one ever told. But I began to avoid going."

Despite the occasional scuffle with bullies, our lives together were full of school projects and sports. I sat happily in the sun at Little League games, chatting with parents, letting an afternoon glide into evening in the timeless pleasure of watching our kids pitch, hit, catch, miss, throw, and occasionally slide. Or, in the depths of a chilled winter, Bill and I stood in the soothing heat of a YMCA pool, acting as timers as our boys swam hard to beat each other and their own best times. Each summer, I hunkered into a canvas chair to read for class-prep as the boys surfed along Narragansett Beach—rocking gently on the green-blue water, waiting patiently for just the right swell, then paddling hard for position, and with luck, rising fast to catch the crest of the wave. I'd walk the long white stretch of sand, calmed by the wide expanse of ocean, the rhythmic surf, and remember walking with my mother along the New Jersey shore, years ago.

With my boys I felt the energy, the humor, and the hopefulness of being young again. They teased me wryly–"Mom, are you talking for the dog again?" Or they grabbed my hand and made me dance to an old R&B song–Elvis Presley, Marvin Gaye. At Sunday dinner prepared by "Barbeque Bill," as we sat together and caught up on the week's events, I felt grateful and content. But the shadow of Geoff's death was always there; he seemed stubbornly determined to rise up into full flesh whenever the universe gave him a tear in the fabric to reenter our lives, remind us he was not to be forgotten.

The inevitable happened when Peter was ten, and in the hospital. At age eight, he had suffered horrible nightmares and doctors found a snarl of veins in his brain that threatened an early stroke. At nine, they zapped it with laser surgery to burn away the snarl. Now, months later, his scorched brain had swelled against his cranium, threatening to squeeze all life from him, and he was pinned in a hospital bed for the third time—tied up with wires all over his head, and being pumped with steroids which, while saving his life by shrinking his brain back to normal, were also swelling his body beyond recognition. He was in fifth grade and furious that he looked as he did, furious that he was going through all these invasions of tubes and needles again, and saying he was going to kill himself. I knew he was tired of pain and that his threat was angry expletive more than real plan. But the doctors sent the psychiatrist over to be sure, and Bill was there to answer his questions.

Later that afternoon, when I came in from teaching, Bill had gone back to work, and Peter was watching TV. I sat down, exhausted, ready to grade some essays while I kept him company, and before I headed home to take care of our other boys.

"Mom, did your brother kill himself?"

I stared at my student's essay. "Yes. Who told you?"

"I heard Daddy on the phone with the doctor. He was explaining that you had this history in your family." Silence. "You said it was an accident. Why didn't you tell me?"

I looked out at that gray March evening from that awful white hospital room where Peter sat, trussed up with hurtful wires that could never tell us all we wanted to know to make him OK, and I felt very, very tired. The tears streamed down onto those forgotten essays, and I told him everything. Or at least I told him the legend—about the Boy Scouts, the Vietnam War, Quakers, his Grampa and Grammy, and pacifism. And suddenly I realized Geoff was sounding like a hero again, making suicide seem like an option in response to frustration. I sat in that hard plastic chair feeling already whipped. I looked right at Peter.

"But Peter, the most important thing is how angry I am at him. I loved him, and I wish from the bottom of my heart that some misguided grown-ups and kids weren't so hard on him. But I'm mostly angry at him because he never realized how what he did would hurt so many of us for so very long."

Peter was quiet for a long time, glowering. "I have his same birthday."

"I know. But it's your birthday. You are you, not him. Don't you ever, ever forget that."

The most brazen attempt I made at staving off the fear of Geoff's legacy came the next year when Peter went into a tailspin after being taunted continuously in middle school for his swollen steroidal face. Sympathetic therapists were no help; they couldn't stop the brutality of schoolyard kids.

"You've got to try and walk away, Pete," I said.

"Oh, please, Mom. This is the real world. If I want to fight them, I will."

"Let me at least talk to the principal."

"Mom." He looked pained. "He can't do anything either. Kids will say anything they want. Or they just wait till you get a few feet off the school grounds and you're fair game."

"Then let me pick you up."

"Right. Let them see me being picked up by Mommy."

"Peter, I can't abide this!" My stomach clenched. His eyes burned into me.

"It isn't your nice little Quaker world anymore, Mom! Kids don't give a shit. If they want to push you around, they will."

"It never was a nice little Quaker world, Peter. But—maybe we should consider a private school for awhile."

"Oh, please. All those spoiled preps. They're just as bad, Mom. They're the kids I know at Boy Scouts. They may be rich kids but they insult you just the same. They just smirk instead of hit."

"Some of their parents seem nice," I said, realizing as I spoke I was revisiting an age-old conversation.

"THEIR PARENTS DON'T SEE, MOM!"

"You know, Pete. You're right. And you know what else? Go ahead and fight back—if you've tried everything else . . . I think I would too."

So Peter's pent-up rage finally burst, and he did fight back, and was suspended for a day. I said, OK, I'm taking you to New York for a day off with Daphne. And we went, distracting ourselves with the pleasure of her embrace and her new art show of quilts, all gaily draped on the walls of the school where she taught.

But, of course, the fight and the time out couldn't stop the inevitability of the bullying. This time kids made jokes in the classroom during discussions when Peter's wounded brain sometimes froze on him, or threw out a word that didn't quite make sense, even though he knew what he was trying to say. Kids called him names in front of others. He came home and slammed the front door.

"It won't work!" he yelled. "Nothing works!" He stomped up the stairs toward his room. "I'm going to kill myself!"

I stood in the hallway, looking up at him, my own brain suddenly frozen. I understood his fury and I wanted to murder those bullies myself. But now, as I heard those words "Kill myself! Kill myself!" I was suddenly screaming at him: "YOU WILL NOT TALK LIKE THAT IN MY HOUSE!"

He stopped short on the stairs, looked down at me, glowering, silent.

"It is just NOT OK, Pete," I said, gritting my teeth, fighting back the tears. "EVER!"

He understood. But I understood, too, that no matter what any of us knows, there will be days when the past or the outside world rushes in to grab us like a poisonous, subterranean monster. There is no way to predict or avoid it. Some of us are born with the toughness to deflect the onslaught. Most of us have to learn self-defense, and must practice—how to hold on to our heart, strengthen our armor, hold at arm's length the unfairness that trips us up, the frustrations that rack us—until our anger deflates, gives us room to figure out a calmer, less destructive game plan. For Peter, solace would slowly begin to come through music. Complicated ragings on drums would lead to jazzy meditations on a keyboard, and over the next few years he would immerse himself in a world of composing and producing that bullies could not touch.

A year after my confrontation with Peter, the poison of Geoff's death rose up again—suddenly, in the midst of an ordinary day of swim team practice and homework. Peter had asked about some line from a Doors song and we were talking about music, the tragedies of the sixties, and I said something about Geoff's suicide, not knowing that ten-year-old Sam had come in to the room. "What do you mean?" he asked. And there it was again. No way out. While Peter had responded to the startling news with anger and worry, Sam just cried and cried, a big heart full of feeling for an uncle he would never know, spilling over without words. Bill came home from work as I was comforting Sam on his bed. I was trying to explain that this was a long time ago, and that Geoff had made his own decision, he had just gone a little nuts, and it didn't have anything to do with us now, except that it still hurt. But Sam wasn't hearing. Peter explained to Bill what had happened as he loomed in the doorway.

"That's enough!" Bill barked, anger pounding in his eyes. "Sam, it was a long time ago, and it has NOTHING to do with you!" Sam tried hard to stifle his sobs under the glare of his father's wrath. I was furious at Bill for his insensitivity that night. But I knew, once again, if his style was abominable, his message got through. Fifteen years earlier he had told me to please get the ghost of my brother out of our bed; he was trying to forge a real marriage. Now he was trying to save his children. I agreed with him: It was a long time ago, and we were trying hard here to create a new life, in a new direction, free and clear of the lingering consequences of Geoff's decision.

In the midst of these years of graduate school, children's play and tussles, ghosts from the past and current tensions, my mother's final trial began. After all her years of caring for us so well, in good health and without complaint, she had developed Parkinson's disease. It crippled her body and stole away the dream of a traveling retirement with my father. For ten years she coped valiantly with her failing body and my father's unpredictable emotions. I felt I was watching her die slowly of the disease of her buried pain—as if all those years of not talking back, or all those years of not forgiving herself for not being able to control Geoff's pain or my pain or any of our pain—all those years had just eaten up her nervous system and drained away all her dopamine, the chemical in her brain that had tried to keep her body and soul together, literally. She was determined to make the best of it. One night, after a day of watching my boys play, she crawled slowly, shakily, into bed and I said, "I don't know how thee can bear this, Mom." She stopped in mid-hunch, willed her head up to look at me and said, "But Bethy, I have so much to live for." It was that simple, and that profound: the pure pleasure of seeing her grandchildren and of being in the same room with a daughter was enough to keep her going. I, in my chronic angst, stood there silenced with admiration.

For my father, watching my mother wither, living with caretakers and medical equipment, life felt intolerable at times. He became

Jekyll and Hyde, creating the occasional family uproar. He would criticize my mother and her neediness; then sit by her bed as she went to sleep, play old folk songs on his harmonica and tell her if he had the chance to do it all over again, he would marry her in a minute. To me he declared that by putting my children in day care as I went through graduate school, I showed that perhaps I didn't love them enough, the implication being that I was a bad mother; then months later he offered to pay for our babysitter Margaret as I wrote my dissertation. When he saw Bill's hands-off style of parenting he growled, "What kind of father are you!" Then months later he offered to help with the down payment for a larger house as our brood grew. My father's view of our sons vacillated too. "They're city boys," he muttered. "Don't know anything about real camping, or cutting wood, and have no interest in soccer, for heaven's sake!" But then he laughed with delight as they showed off their swimming prowess in the pool at Bryn Gweled, or drew for him a complex illustration of a Model T, or played "My Country, 'Tis of Thee" on the harmonicas he had given them and taught them to play.

One evening, my father took us outside to sit in the summer twilight at Tobacco Road and he told the boys the story of Monarch the Big Bear. My boys listened to their craggy old grandpa with respect, like he was a curious throwback to some ancient time.

"So, Monarch," my father said, his strong hand tapping the arm of his wooden lawn chair as he looked out over the trees that now enclosed the bottom of the terrace slope.

"A bear bigger than any man had ever seen. Way out there in the Colorado Rocky Mountains. When he stood on his hind legs in anger, or to sniff the air, or to sense an enemy, he towered over a man, almost two times his height. Monarch was known by every hunter in the region. He had killed a rancher's cattle, and he had killed a man with one swipe of his huge paw.

"Hunters had shot at him—three, four, who knows how many bullets had gone into him. One hunter saw him go down, crashing to the earth so it shook. But when the hunter got closer, to see if Monarch was down for good, the bear reared up suddenly and stared down at that hunter with his beady, furious eyes so the hunter just stood there, frozen, unable to move his gun. Monarch growled, from deep in his shaggy throat, a menacing, unearthly disgust. Then he limped off into the woods, crushing the underbrush, dismissing the hunter.

"Some hunters said, it wasn't worth pursuing him; just let him live his legendary life. But as the mountains became more settled, and roads brought more people, the legend of Monarch the Big Bear brought bounty hunters, men who cared nothing for the laws of nature or the respect for the long-lived king of all bears. A group of them joined forces, made nets and traps, and set up an ambush that finally brought old Monarch down. Slashing at the net, caught by a dumbly strong rope, Monarch screamed his insulted fury one more time as the bounty-hunters pumped him with high-powered rifles, again and again and again, until . . . there was silence."

My boys and I listened, entranced, moved not only by the power of Monarch, but by my father's passion, drama, and belief. He saw that bear right in front of him, he gestured high into the air toward its height, and he laid that bear down to rest gently, as if he knew him well, he understood him, and he knew that his time was gone forever. I knew my boys would never hear this story in their computerized, Nintendoed lives where, in the 1990s, the oldest stories on school reading lists came from the 1960s. But a few years later, when the movie *Legends of the Fall* passed through our VCR, we watched, fascinated, as a huge, brown grizzly reared up and loomed threateningly over Brad Pitt, alone in the pine-choked wilderness. "That's Grampa's Monarch," Sam said quietly. His brothers nodded, their eyes glued to the power of the old, shaggy beast.

Mom and Dad in their elder years.

Faith

As I watched my mother's slow-burn death, battled off and on with my father, negotiated differences with Bill, and helped my sons face the trials of life, I began to understand I was no longer a Quaker. There came a day when I woke up in the pit again, with children needing me, classes to attend, and I felt as empty and alone as I had ever been. No equation of occasional therapy or sympathetic friends or children's hugs had taken that pit away. I had started drinking again at night, after the kids were in bed, and was trying hard to ignore the familiar exhaustion of sobering up after each hangover, knowing I would have to stop.

Now I was lying there, unable to move, helplessly pinned and surrounded by silence, once again. I lay there for what seemed a long time, although I know at that point in my life there was never a long period of time to lie anywhere. And then something happened that I could not explain. After many minutes of absolute nothingness—no breathing, no sense of my body, just an utter hopelessness, as if I were dead even as I lived, a feeling came slowly up from my belly into my chest and head that was warm and lifting; and then it seemed to swirl suddenly out of me and back into me like a large floating presence of life and energy and comfort, mostly of comfort, like being with one's dearest friend in the world; but this was no one I knew personally, and he—it felt like a he—just swooped down and I felt myself lifted, held, and comforted. He stayed there with me, just holding me up, for what seemed another long time; and then I wondered if I had come as close as I ever would to feeling what some said the presence of Christ might feel like.

I had had glimpses of mystical experiences since I was a child– in Quaker Meeting reveries, upon waking, when walking alone on beaches. A vision or memory or thought would become almost three-dimensional and I would come to, so to speak, in the middle of it. Afterwards I would feel changed, almost disoriented. But this was different. It reminded me of the deeply dark nights in the year after Geoff died, when I would suddenly feel that I had lost all mooring, that I had been ripped away from all connections and from anything that made sense. This time, though, I hadn't had to shake myself out of my own dread. Nor had I drawn willfully on some kind of Inner Light as I did the first time I stopped drinking. Whatever this comfort was, it had come without bidding. Bill, a longtime lover of operatic plotlines, decided I had come to a moment like Mary at the foot of the cross, and like Mary I had been lifted, and told it would be all right. But before I could even tell Bill about an experience I knew he and no one in my politically correct graduate school could fathom with any seriousness, I had to find my own ways to understand why I was still so deeply conflicted and what had just happened to me.

My graduate seminars offered some guidance. I began to see clues to my own dilemmas in the philosophical debates of the eighteenth century: was man evil at heart or good? Quaker belief was built on the sentimental tradition: man was good at heart, inherently an angel, spoiled only by experience. Thus the task of life and religion was to nurture the good, to follow the light within, and to avoid the society of corrupters. The Puritan tradition of the early colonies believed that man was corrupt at heart; he needed religious society to rule, contain, control, make manageable each individual's essentially evil nature.

One day I discovered Hawthorne's short story, "Gentle Boy." The title said "Geoff" in my mind, and the plot played out those eighteenth-century debates. Puritan kids in the 1650s persecuted a Quaker boy. His father had been hung, his mother banished into the woods for preaching their heresies in public. Their body-quaking rants extolled individual faith in the Inner Light over any authority, be it the literal Bible or government. The Quaker boy was taken in by a Puritan couple, who promised to love him as their own. But the villagers believed he was the Devil's child. Children pummeled him with sticks and pelted him with stones. He survived long enough to greet his mother on her return from exile. But he died of a weak heart before he could see her being tolerated by her stern Puritan neighbors. I noted Hawthorne's warning: this Quaker boy was too sensitive. "When trodden upon, he would not turn; when wounded, he could but die. His mind was wanting in the stamina for self-support . . ." Like Geoff. Like me right now in this demanding time of my life.

In such moral fiction I felt strangely affirmed, feeling it offered clues–that Geoff's story, my struggles with Quaker idealism and Bill's puritanical judgments, were rooted in a historical tension. Thinking about Geoff and his own struggles with anger, I realized I had never heard a Quaker use the word "sin," or talk about a need for forgiveness. We had no vocabulary to talk openly about violent feelings or abuse in our own lives. It was just presumed that we were good, gentle, pacifistic, altruistic; any urges to the contrary were our own private shame. Now, in my marriage, Quaker me always assumed the best of people until they proved otherwise–the sentimental optimist; Bill, raised and educated in Puritan New England, always assumed the worst and was skeptical of goodness—the cynical pessimist. Every disagreement we had came down to this difference. Together we worked to understand the truth was somewhere in between.

In another seminar it was Flannery O'Connor—a very Catholic writer, and thus from the tradition my childhood self had seen as ignorant—who showed me what I was ready to understand about faith despite such tension. In her stories goodness evaporates through thoughtless habit, or it is shocked awake by evil. On the surface, her tales can read like social realism more than religious tales; her references to Christ, metaphorical. She knew readers like me, and all my liberal academic friends, did not see belief in Christ as a matter of life or death. For such readers, the hero of her novel *Wise Blood* is a hero because he tries so hard to escape from his religious background, to be an anti-Christ. But, O'Connor said, in her mind, he is a hero because he can NOT get rid of "the ragged figure who moves from tree to tree in the back of his mind." That ragged figure is Christ, she said. The inevitability of that figure is grace. For me that ragged figure was suddenly palpable; it was here, lurking behind my layers of buried sadnesses—as grieving sister, as failed lover, now as worn-out student-wife-and-mother. It was my Christ that I had no rational control over, that I could not explain away no matter how educated I became, and that I could not reject because He was just there, picking me up, holding me, offering solace no matter what I thought.

I decided I needed to find out what a church would feel like to me now. I had not been to Quaker Meeting for years. My own struggles with anger made me suspicious of the professional goodness of Quakers in general. I told my children stories of Quakers' history and their roles in wars, but I chose not to teach them the plain language. I let my parents and sister offer it instead, and the boys enjoyed the thee-thy-thine as what it was, an arcane, endearing habit in my family. For myself, I wanted a new spiritual place, a new home that fit the person I had become. It had to be a church where I felt unpressured, but which enjoyed a reasonable sense of the biblical narrative. Quaker Meetings had offered the occasional biblical quote, but most speakers offered secular musings on peace and current events, Quaker history and love. As my sister said, "We didn't grow up learning the Bible; we grew up learning pacifism and the Vietnam War."

I longed for the camaraderie of Quaker Meeting, the comfort of shared spiritual searching. But I also wanted intelligent appreciation of the oldest story ever told—the story I had come to see writers were always rewriting in their own terms and eras: of how we crucify the messenger, or those we love, and how we never learn from it, and how all we can do is ask forgiveness, again and again and again. As Doctor Parcival says in Sherwood Anderson's *Winesburg, Ohio*, "We are all Christ, and we are all crucified." And, as Faulkner and Flannery O'Connor reminded us, we easily become the crucifiers—usually in the name of a religion or philosophy. I was beginning to see the danger of orthodoxy in all walks of life—in my Quaker past, in religion in general, even in the scholarly debates of the academy, where a new guard of theorists was dethroning an old guard of historians. Always, the current "right" way of thinking quickly deteriorated into mean-spirited arrogance and blinding presumption. I wanted a break, a rebirth, to feel that ancient place in me that had been drowned out by the cacophony of my loud, clashing adult life. It was a place of feeling and knowing that started before, and transcended all, my logic and education. I had felt it again in the spirit that had swirled into and out of me in my inexplicable reverie. I wanted to find a place where I could make sense of that, then hold on to its comfort and wisdom.

After a few tries in various Protestant churches—too stiff; too loose; too paternal—I finally found my berth in the church that had banished Quakers from Massachusetts. I vaguely assumed Congregationalists would be an upper-middle-class bunch of conservatives. But in Providence I found a congregation where liberal optimism seemed as welcome as conservative constraint. The young woman minister moved easily from scripture to literature to real-life anecdote with an intelligence and pragmatism that still embraced an unabashed belief in the palpable presence of God.

In one sermon, Rebecca described how Ann Beattie's characters seemed to watch passively as life came at them, tossed them around, passed them by, left them as empty at the end as at the start. What was Beattie getting at? Was this an enervated version of turning the other cheek? Must pacifism be passive? What about the inevitable fights in a marriage? Even a good marriage. What about unfairness at work or injustice toward a group? Can turning the other cheek disintegrate into resignation, a kind of nonliving? How can we survive the compromises and wounds of life without lying down or giving up? What are the moments that wake us up, recharge our hearts? Perhaps it's in those moments that we know grace. Perhaps in those moments we see the unpredictable possibilities of faith. I listened to this young, smart woman and I felt I fit. So I stayed.

In that church, as I began to sing hymns again, I felt the spirit of my Grandmother Plaisted, remembered her singing as she stared blindly into the air, earnestly holding the arms of her rocking chair, her aging voice wavering at first, then gaining confidence as she sang, "Our God, our help in ages past . . ." I imagined her as a young woman, holding her hymnbook as she stood in her Baptist church in Sanford, Maine, and then I saw my mother as a teenager beside her; I could feel them now, each of them within me, beside me, strong in their faith and endurance.

Sometimes sermons felt familiar from my Quaker past. "The light shines in the darkness and the darkness does not overcome it." But unlike Quaker practice, I heard words that acknowledged the abuses

of life out loud, beyond the Lord's Prayer, in a shared prayer of confession; together, we asked for mercy, and for the ability to forgive
others–every week. Mercy. To forgive. I had been trying on my own
for years to save myself from the poisoning effects of frustration and
anger. Now the words and the belief in this church felt like they might
actually help me do it. My Sunday mornings became my solace, my
time-out, my space to return to the faithfulness of my youth, but in a
way that spoke directly to the challenges of my present.

In July of 1995 I drove the boys down for their summer visit with
my parents. My mother sat in the living room, confined to a mechani-
cal chair with tubes connected to a machine to help her lungs work.
Each day we buzzed around her–helping her caretaker Nancy, running
errands, finding snacks, taking walks around Bryn Gweled, or heading
for the pool, then reporting back to her after each adventure.

One morning, the sun shone brilliantly through the big picture
window as my mother looked out over the lawn that sloped down
to the trees near the garden now choked with weeds, and the blackberry and grape arbors beyond. As I packed snacks and towels into a
backpack for the kids, I looked up and saw my mother pulling out the
tubes holding her down. I stood transfixed. She waved at my youngest
boy, five-year-old Max, who was drawing at the old tea table by the
window.

"Max," she said hoarsely. She waved him toward her and he looked
scared. Her bent frame and frail arms seemed alien to him.

"It's OK, Max," I said. "Grammy needs your help." He slid off the
chair and padded over to my mother, watching her intently, shyly,
as she pulled her walker toward her and pushed mightily to get up.
Nancy came into the room and we each took quick, long steps, ready
to grab her elbows.

"I'm OK," my mother said, her voice thin but firm. "Max, let's go."
He looked at me. I raised my eyebrows, smiled at him encouragingly.
I had no idea what was up. She stood, resting on her walker a bit till
she got her legs back.

My mother clumped into the kitchen on her walker, followed by a
tentative Max. "A pot, Max," I heard my mother say. He must not have
understood her weak voice. "Pot," she said again.

I didn't follow to help. She hadn't walked like this in days. If she asked so specifically for Max, I knew she had a plan meant just for him.

In the kitchen, I heard some pots clang, then some shuffling, then my mother's slow clump, clump, clump down the basement stairs. Then, Max's softer, small steps.

I looked out the window and saw my mother reappear down by the basement door, heading for the lower lawn. With each step, she tossed the walker forward and followed it, tossed it forward and followed it.

Nancy and I stared in disbelief out the window.

"How is she breathing?" I said.

"I don't know." Nancy looked at me, smiling thoughtfully. "But clearly she knows what she's doing."

I watched my mother reach the arbor and point to where the ripest blackberries always grew. Max reached his thin arms up to a patch and wrapped his fist around some. She raised her head from its hunch and said something to him. Gently, he pulled.

On the last morning of our visit, my mother took longer than usual to get dressed for breakfast. We were all sitting, waiting for her at the table in the living room, when she finally entered, steady on her walker, her hair neatly combed back in her usual bun, wearing her favorite turquoise dress and her favorite brooch. She had put on bright red lipstick. Nancy smiled, holding her elbow. "She wanted to look her best for you!" My mother smiled, almost shyly, at us. My boys and I grinned at her. And then I paused. In that moment I knew what my mother knew, why she had dressed up for us. I caught her eye, held back the tears.

Early in August, Dad, Daphne and I walked toward the big old tree that sheltered Geoff and my cousin Rick in the graceful expanse of the cemetery of the Abington Meeting House. Moving slowly in the bright summer sun, I cradled the elegant coolness of a ceramic urn and within it the incredible lightness of my mother's ashes. I gently lowered it into the square-shaped hole, nestled the ceramic roundness into the dark, fresh earth. As I rose, gazed at the delicately glazed top of her urn, I suddenly felt palpably a flow of relief. I knew, in that moment, we were burying with her, forever, the heaviest sorrow of losing Geoff.

"OK, Mom," I said quietly. The end of her sadness seemed so clear and releasing. "It's OK now." The three of us stood, silently looking down at the beauty of her urn, knowing it held room for my father to come.

There in the quiet and the heat, standing with Dad and Daphne under the big, old tree, I thought of Mom and Max, three weeks earlier, down by the blackberries. And then I saw another August morning, more than thirty years before—very early, the windows of Tobacco Road all open, not a breeze. I awoke to hear my mother's clear laugh outside somewhere. As I headed sleepily for the bathroom, I looked out the window and saw my mother with Geoff, quietly picking blueberries in the early morning coolness. No one else awake—just Mom and Geoff, out by the blueberry bushes down our long drive, sharing their early-bird pleasures, some quiet joke of Geoff's. Plunk . . . Plunk . . . the blueberries falling into their pans.

The next day every bench in the Meeting House was filled with friends and family who told stories of my mother's kindness, her mentoring, her open-hearted hug, her creative projects, and her skill as an organizer. I had been thinking about faith, and the legacy of hope passed down from my Grandmother Plaisted in Maine to my mother, to us. I told the story of the runaway horse in the winter of 1916 and how my grandmother prayed as she tossed my bundled mother into a snowbank. "I will always see my mother's legacy in that image of my grandmother," I said, "sailing after my infant mother into the cold winter air. In the face of such madness—a terrified horse, Geoffy's death, Parkinson's disease, my mother, like her mother before her, was unpretentiously brave."

A year after my mother died, my father and I sat in the living room at Tobacco Road on a summer night, after my boys had gone to bed out in the tent we had set up for them. It was time to talk of many things, but first, Geoff. We didn't talk about him much anymore. Grandchildren, Daphne's and my adult lives, my parents' elderly illnesses, had filled our times together. I was talking to old friends and family about Geoff, trying to write an essay, and I needed to know what my father understood after all these years. He looked tired, slumped in his old armchair by the fireless hearth, his dirty, worn baseball cap now a part of him, even in the house, as cancer began to eat away his life force.

"I have spent thousands of nights thinking about Geoffy," he said. "Trying to figure out some clear clue. I have a considerable sense of guilt about what I might have done to help him."

"What might thee have done?" I asked.

"Go to that Boy Scout meeting, maybe. Or love him more."

"In what way?"

"I always tucked Daphne and thee into bed and sang each of you a song. But I never did with Geoff . . . For some reason I thought it would make him feel self-conscious."

"But thee did say good night to him."

"Yes. Yes, I did. And, on the other hand, if any of you three children were spoiled, Geoff was the spoiled one, by me and I think by Mother. I spent more time with him—took him on camping trips, took him skiing, took him on his eighth birthday for a day hike and picnic with two of his friends . . ."

I nodded, remembering my envy.

"But," my father said, "I, like my father, did expect more from an only son than from daughters—a fact I'm a little ashamed of now."

"That was quite a legacy thee inherited from thy father, and that thee handed on to Geoff," I said.

"Yes, it was." He paused, watching me, knowing I was fishing for some acknowledgment of something from him, some confession.

I knew I would never have another chance to be so frank with him. "Does thee ever think maybe it was all just too much for Geoff?" I asked.

"Thee means our family history? Our Quakerism?" He searched for my meaning.

I wasn't sure what I wanted. "Like that argument you two had the night he died–"

"I wouldn't call it an argument," my father said. "I'd say, more a disagreement."

"I remember him as very upset," I said. "I remember feeling like thee was just pushing him too hard with thy desire to have him talk about our family."

"I remember it more as I offered a suggestion and he didn't care for it," my father said.

I wondered, was he just humanly editing the memory or had I exaggerated mine? "Did thee ever wonder did thee push him too hard?" I persisted.

"No." My father shook his head once. "As I said, I have thought about Geoffy—and why, over and over and over–countless nights lying awake. And I don't see that my personality hurt him, or that our beliefs hurt him."

"Some people think otherwise," I said, and stopped, scared of my own boldness, but also egged on by it. "Some people think Geoff was sort of suffocated by our family expectations, particularly thine–the whole male, Quaker, Haverford, gentleman-scholar-athlete, C.O. thing."

He studied me, perhaps working hard not to lash back at my challenge. But he stayed calm, carefully choosing his words. Both of us knew that this conversation had to go right.

"I'm well aware that I have a strong personality," he said. "But I honestly believe that it had nothing to do with Geoff's death. I still believe it was the Boy Scout leaders who were the most responsible for his death."

I stared past my father's shadowy form in the armchair, out at the dark evening, soft and damp as it oozed through the screen windows at the sides of the huge picture window. I wondered if I had just come full circle with my father, if there was just nowhere left to go. But then, my father told me some things I didn't know.

"I have thought sometimes," he said, "that maybe there's a genetic weakness that Geoff inherited." He paused, thinking it through again. "There were two distant cousins of mine who committed suicide, when we were younger. One of them did, apparently, have abuse, or neglect, at home. But the other, I'm not quite sure–his family was very loving, successful–farmers and teachers."

I knew about this second one. I had grown up with his nieces and nephews, my third cousins, playing at family and school reunions. I remembered, when I was in high school, asking their mother, the sister of the young man who had hung himself in their barn, when did she finally get over it? "Well, you don't," she said. "But it gets easier to live with. Over time. Having children helps."

Yes, having children, I knew now, made all the difference. I sat up a bit in my chair. This possibility of a genetic link was intriguing, if also a bit frightening.

"Sometimes," my father said, "when thinking about Geoff, I have thought back to a story Dottie told me about her father, thy Grampa Plaisted. One day when he and Grammy were away from their house in Maine, two boys from across the street came over and ate most of the grapes on Grampa's little grape arbor—about twelve or fifteen feet long. Since they were boys, it's quite understandable how they would eat them all–gorge on them.

"Grampa was very hurt–he was more hurt than angry. So, what did he do? Did he go and talk to the father and confront the boys with it? No. He went and cut down the whole grape arbor. This was a grown man, well into his forties. He took it out on himself."

"Did he ever act like that again?" I asked.

"Not that I know of."

Bizarre, I thought. But it's enough to make one wonder if there is a gene, or a malformation of a gene, that twists the chemical route of anger away from appropriate outlets, and diverts it toward oneself.

My father adjusted his body a bit in the big old armchair, gazed into the dark of the fireplace. "Geoffy," he said, "was more like mother and her father, Grampa—kind and accommodating, by nature gentle. Perhaps, in Geoff's case, to a fatal fault."

"Did thee see clues to that genetic link in Geoff as a boy?" I asked.

"Well, perhaps. One thing. When he was in kindergarten, his teacher told us that in Geoff's drawings and paintings there were no arms. Then, the teacher discovered that another boy had been biting Geoff, and that Geoff had not fought back or told the teacher. So the teacher said, 'Now Geoff, next time you're going to bite back.' And Geoff bit the boy on the arm."

My father paused and looked at me. "Such advice would not pass muster with the school board now, of course. But, guess what came back? The arms and hands. He suddenly felt empowered not to have to take that biting from another person."

I nodded, stared into the dark fireplace. I thought of my son Peter, fighting back against the bullies when he was ill that spring. I thought of Daphne and my discussions about our mother–how each of us had to learn not to shove hurt or unfairness down into our stomachs as she did. I thought of my arguments with Bill–how we had learned over time to channel frustration into new behavior instead of painful wound.

Exhausted now, my father and I sat silently, letting the quiet of the night fold around us, soothe us, as if in Quaker Meeting, until finally there was no more need for words.

Two summers later, I took my boys down to visit my father for his favorite holiday, the Fourth of July. I knew the cancer was having its final sway. But he would have none of it. "Ready for a swim, boys?" he said as we unfolded our stiff bodies from the car and the long drive down from Providence. "Yeah!" they said. The boys and I quickly changed into our swimsuits, and waited patiently as my father changed into his cut-off jeans and walked carefully out to the car, balancing with his cane, his body now shrunken from the ravages of chemotherapy. "I used to be strong, boys," he said as they watched him negotiate the small step down from the porch to the gravel. "I used to out-run every boy on the football field–I was small, but fast . . ." He stopped and leaned on his cane. "Ahh, to be down there at the ten-yard line, the odds all against you, and you take them on . . . That's how I am, boys. I'm down at the ten-yard line, but I'm still fighting." My boys were ready to dive into the Bryn Gweled pool to entertain my father with a mock swimming race. But as we entered the pool gates, my father walked firmly to the bench, greeted the scattered neighbors sitting about, dropped his cane and towel, turned and dove confidently into the pool–like a healthy, young man. All of us watched, amazed, and then, as he popped up out of the water and whooped, we grinned.

The next night, I awoke with a start to hear my father crying, somewhere in the darkness, downstairs. I had seen him cry as he evoked memories of Geoff—intense, fleeting moments of sorrow. But this was different, like an animal wail of despair caused by unbearable physical pain. In the hospital it would take ten more days for his body to give up, and in those days, as the good estate lawyer he was, he dictated the steps we would need to follow to settle his affairs, noting who would take care of what, and which keys were where. On one of my final nights with him, alone, we talked about the writing I was doing about Geoff. He had seen a draft and was upset about how he was portrayed at times, and that I had mixed up some historical facts about Quakers. I sat next to him as he lay in his bed. Both of us felt bad for having to talk about this now. Part of me was so worn down by these years of dying that I just wanted this to be over. But I said, "Dad, when I rewrite these stories, I promise I will rewrite with thy voice in my head."

He nodded slightly. "It's thy story to tell."

His attempt at generosity, even as he lay withered with pain, unnerved me. Suddenly my adult defenses let down, my exhaustion sliced through the big daughter caretaker, ripped me open right back to my twelve-year-old self, and I started to cry.

"I just wish we could KNOW, Dad," I blurted. "I just wish–I wish there was somebody to BLAME!" I stopped short, embarrassed, shamed by my regression.

He gazed weakly at me. "We'll never know, Bethy," he whispered. "We'll never know."

I took my boys back to their summer plans and Daphne came down to be with our father. She sat with him during the day and at night she laid out a new quilt on the living-room floor of our silent childhood home. Where once we built wood-block houseboats and set tables for parties, she distracted her sorrow with a design she had felt after I called. Now, sleepless, in the eerie quiet of the house, she arranged pieces of gold, yellow, white, surrounded by darkness—blues, browns, and greens; smooth silk from old Japanese kimonos shining against rough cotton, linen, and muslin—building steps of gold into a tower of light, despite the darkness.

At dawn the nurse called to say, come now, and Daphne asked Nancy, my parents' faithful caretaker, to join her for the ride. He had been waiting, the nurse said. He had said "no" to the painkillers that morning, so he could stay alert. Daphne took my father's hand and they said the things that needed to be said. Then, after awhile, he looked toward the window, said, "It's a sunny day, honey. Why doesn't thee go out for a little walk. It's OK, Nancy's here." So Daphne went out to stand a bit in the warmth of the July sun, and when she returned, Nancy sat, crying, holding my father's stilled hand. "He watched you go," she said. "He just followed you—out into the sunlight."

A few weeks later, my father's faithful friends–all Quaker classmates, cousins, and Bryn Gweled neighbors—filled a tent on the lawn of Abington Meeting under a blazing sun to remember my father. Daphne read a love note my mother had written to him when she first went into the hospital, saying, "This is all part of life," telling him he was a good husband and he had been a good father. I read Keats's "To Autumn" in honor of what I knew was one of his finest gifts to me—the power and beauty of words, how they moved and uplifted, clarified the present and opened the gates to the past. I recalled his gravelly bass voice reciting at the dinner table: "Where are the songs of Spring? Aye, where are they? / Think not of them, thou hast thy music too."

There was hardly a moment of silence in my father's memorial service. Friends and family shared affectionate, funny, and appreciative stories of his generosity, his humor, his gentlemanly ways, and his joie de vivre. I thought of the scene in James Baldwin's "Notes of a Native Son," when Baldwin says he does not recognize the man being eulogized as his father; and I appreciated Baldwin's observation that in the end each one of us wants to be remembered with charity; it is our best traits we want recalled, because all of us have fallen short of who we wanted to be and it was painful. In death, my father had looked so frail and small, I wanted to reach down, lift him to me and hold him. Now in the embrace of his friends—many of whom had loved him, foibles and all, for a long, long time, I could be moved by the power of my father's spirit and I could finally understand why he had said at the end that if he had the choice, he would live his life all over again—even the sad parts—because "It's been a great ride." Perhaps the searingly truest moment of his memorial came when his cousin Sam stood, bent in the Pennsylvania heat, held on to the tent pole, and after recalling ways in which my father had been a good lawyer and friend, suddenly stopped, wiped his brow, said, "And then, I will always remember—losing Geoff—" He paused, choked, said, "I cry even now—we must never forget."

We don't forget. Not Geoff, nor the war that became inextricably intertwined with our grief and sadness at losing him, then Rick. Soon after my father died, the intense feelings of that time came roaring back as Robert McNamara visited my campus. It was 1999 and policy historians were hosting the former defense secretary as he introduced his most recent book on the lessons of the Vietnam War. I forced myself to go, even though I associated this man with the insidious acceptance of the war, his businesslike visage burned into all of our minds from countless TV interviews and newspaper articles trying to justify the perceived threats to our nation.

Now he was an old man, about my father's age, and as I watched him, I felt such ambivalence. I had read his book *In Retrospect*, and a part of me admired his attempt to ask forgiveness. Living with Bill, the policy maker, I knew how stressful and ethically complicated such jobs could be: analyzing statistics and probabilities, using theoretical constructs and field observations to make intelligent guesses that one hoped had a better-than-50-percent chance of being right, or at least effective. But now, as McNamara calmly answered questions about lost moments when the war might have been stopped, I began to feel the old sorrows rush up into my throat. I realized this could never be an academic subject for me. As in my final visit alone with my father, I suddenly dropped back into my younger self. These detached questions about policy were not about long-ago history, but were here again, now—immediate and horrific. "If we'd only known Ho Chi Minh really wanted peace then, we could have . . ." "If Johnson had only gotten that one memo, then maybe . . ." The war could have been diverted at least three times BEFORE 1965.

BEFORE Geoff decided to pack it in.

Before Butch was killed in a meadow of Vietnam.

Before Tony left the country.

Before Rick decided he HAD to go to Quang Ngai.

Now I was yelling in my head: All these "What ifs!" No thank you,

Mr. McNamara! For every young man and family whose life was changed by that war, No thank you!

Of course I said nothing. I left, thinking about the young men in that room–students of politics, packing the seats, their rapt faces admiring the power this old man once held. Once again it seemed the soldiers and the victims of that awful war had been upstaged by the old boys and their rationalizations. McNamara went on with his national book tour, doing the best he could to say mea culpa. As if it could bring back any body, or heal any psyche, or keep any administration from creating such a tragedy again.

We don't forget. But we do try to move on. In 1999 I started teaching a writing course around the literatures of the Vietnam War. At first the students were children of peace activists and soldiers, Vietnamese mothers and GI dads. Then, Sarath, from Cambodia, and Pang, from Laos, walked in. I realized we would no longer study just the writings of the Vietnam War, but also those of the American War as told by the refugees from Southeast Asia. In the third class, almost all the students came from Vietnam, Cambodia, or Laos and their families were managing the transition to American lives despite the memories of loved ones killed, reeducation camps, children lost along the escape route, starvation, illness, and poverty. I looked around the seminar table at these young men and women and I felt such hope. Here they were in an American university–healthy, capable, alive with plans. They knew what their parents had gone through; they felt the sacred weight of expectations upon them and they were undaunted. They were in this class to understand and honor what their parents lost, and they were the truest proof anyone could have that it was possible to become OK, no matter what the sins of the past.

We don't forget. Soon after my parents died, Daphne and I sat in her living room, high up in her Tribeca apartment, looking out over Manhattan as the evening lights came on. I set my tea down on the round kitchen table that once held our family gatherings at Tobacco Road. Down the hall, in her bedroom, sat the troll house Geoff built for her a year before he died. Its miniature furniture, quilts, fire in the fireplace, screened windows, bark roof, railed stairs, and braided rugs were a bit faded, but still intact thirty-five years later.

For years Daphne has taught art at Friends Seminary, a Quaker school nearby, as she creates richly colored, wall-length quilts that look like abstract paintings. Every few years, she helps her students design, build, paint, and sew tiny quilts for a dollhouse, a life-like model of a Victorian or country house, which they proudly display and auction at her school's fund-raiser.

Settled into my father's old law office chairs, we talked about Quakerism and Geoff, how perhaps our religion and loss led to more soul-searching in our lives, but also to a kind of low-level anxiety.

On the other hand, Daphne said, the legacy of Geoff's death for her was a love of life, an intensity in her art. "That might not have happened if . . ." She stopped.

That "If." If he hadn't died. How awful and strange. I understood—there were gifts from his death. A kind of perspective. A clarity, as my mother once said, about what was important, what was not. An ease with sadness.

Daphne tried again. "Our family seemed so settled in its plans and values. If Geoff hadn't died—" She searched for words. "I might have lived a more middle-of-the-road life—married a Quaker boy, done some art on the side. But his death was such a shock—it threw a lump of aloneness into my throat—I still can't swallow it, I can't digest it; it's always there, it can't be purged—and it didn't allow for that middle-of-the road life."

In my mind, I saw her light-filled studio in Maine, with its small wood stove, down the grassy path from the cabin she shares in summers with Gilbert, her architect husband.

The important thing, she said, is that "I never felt like a victim of any of this—of Geoff's death, or of our family dynamics, or of grief. I always felt I had a choice—despair or fight."

Outside, far across the darkness, lights drew our gazes to distant windows of high-rises, people in living rooms or offices open late.

"The hardest thing has been these long years of Mom and Dad's dying, before their time really, as if Geoff's death aged them faster." She sighed.

Daphne and me posed back to back,
echoing our childhood portrait.

The dollhouse Geoff built for Daphne.

"It's good those stresses are gone. But there's always stress. If I get down or tired now, I'll tell myself, 'Get your ducks in order!' So I'll go do my yoga, or get a massage, or meditate. But silence is best–the time to be silent–and a great pedicure!" She smiled, wiggling her bright red toenails at me.

We don't forget. One day in 2004, I breezed into our family computer room to check my email for student drafts. On Max's keyboard next to mine I saw a handwritten column of words on a well-worn page from a notebook. I was so struck by his writing anything by hand, I picked it up, pleased that he was trying out poetry.

I read the first line. "Yo, what's the point of life when everybody just commits suicide?"

My heart stalled. This was the sunniest of our boys, the comedian of the family. I had never talked to Max about Geoff, but suddenly the ghost was there again. I willed myself to stay calm, keep reading.

> We all hate each other 'spite peace treaties and
>   Benetton ads
> . . .
> All these Islamic nations
> Killing in the name of all that is holy
> . . .
> Innocent bystanders watch and mourn
> Their thoughts are torn–for the remorse, for the
>   forgotten forlorn

So, this was his take on the post-9/11 world. The teacher in me saw this was good writing for a thirteen-year-old. But my heart hung on the rage:

> I dispatch ethnic armies upon the universe
> Disturbing brain waves like Satanists at church
> Visit God at his work
> Rip it up!
> . . .
> Bow down to the warlord!
> Devil may cry but the angels are the slayers,

the decayers
They retreat to the heavens
For a feast of the gods
Tearing up flesh and bone of their creations
. . .

What had initiated this torrent? I distracted myself in my work until he came in to do homework.

"It's just a rap lyric," he said.

"But Max, it's so dark. Do you really feel this angry and cynical?"

He paused, studied me. "No, not really. It's just words, Mom. Don't worry."

I let it lie. But I kept watch.

Two years later, Max and I were sitting on a bench in the early spring sun, enjoying the lawn and trees at Bill's brother's house, waiting for cousins to arrive for Easter dinner.

"Nice out here," I said.

"Reminds me of Grampa and Grammy's house," Max said. "But you can still hear traffic here."

"You could hear the train at Grammy and Grampa's house," I said. "My father LOVED the trains. Their power, their long, shrill whistles. 'There goes the six - oh - five!' he'd say."

"Did you have model trains?" Max asked.

"Yes," I said, suddenly alert. "My brother built a whole train landscape in the basement–tunnels, hills, a little town. Daphne and I loved to go down and watch the train swoosh around in circles, over a bridge, even let out smoke. Lionel trains–this big." I showed him with my hands.

"Sometimes I wish I had another uncle," Max said.

I paused. "You mean Geoff," I said.

"Yes."

"I know. I wish you did too."

We were silent for a bit. "We haven't talked much about that, have we," I said.

"I kinda knew."

"Peter and Sam tell you?"

"Yeah, a while back."

"It's hard to talk about. It's just so sad."

"Grampa said that too."

"He did?" I was incredulous. I had no idea my father had mentioned Geoff's death to the boys. I had made him promise to let me be the one who initiated or fielded the subject of his suicide.

"Yeah, on his deathbed–when he asked you to go out of the hospital room so he could talk to us alone."

That was the day after my own tears with my father, the last time we saw him. "What did Grampa say?" I asked.

"That it was a shame your brother did that to himself. I didn't understand then. I was seven. I thought maybe he had gone into the Army or something. I knew he had died."

We sat quietly.

"Do you have questions?" I said.

"Just, 'why.' It's so . . . extreme."

"Yes. It was."

Max looked toward me. "We don't have to—." Concern softened his voice.

"It's OK. I was twelve, Daphne was ten. We didn't know why either. We just asked everyone we knew. He had been a straight A student, president of his school, really good at soccer. Some said maybe it was the time–many people were still for the Vietnam War then—1964, '65. He was being beaten up at school, and pushed around at Boy Scouts, because he talked about his beliefs—against the war, and people thought we were weird, being Quakers and living in a community where we all owned the land together–called us Communist. But even that doesn't explain why. We'll never know."

I felt calm, peaceful, aware I was being cryptic with the familiar script but feeling it was enough. We sat quietly, our faces warm in the sun.

After a few minutes Max said, "That rap I wrote a while back–about what's the point of life–you were upset, I felt bad. It was after Peter told me–it's what I felt thinking about your brother."

I turned to him. "Max, I had no idea. I'm sorry—"

"I felt bad. But I did feel dark," Max said.

"We all do sometimes," I said.

"I've been thinking about adult life–you know, in that big way– what it's all worth. Some Mondays I just wonder, why am I doing this. And later I realize, well, there's things I like–music, friends."

"I get most dark in the middle of the night," I said. "Over time I've learned, just wait, within twenty-four hours things almost always get better." I looked over at him. "You make me better–you make me laugh."

"That's my steez, Moms." He smiled sideways at me.

"What's that mean?" I started to smile.

"That's my *style*, Mom."

As we sat there, quiet for a bit, I imagined all the times my children have hurt and I didn't know it. I reminded myself I'm supposed to let go, have faith that, like their imperfect parents, they too will figure it all out somehow. One of Peter's doctors said to me, long after Peter was healed, lean, and functioning well, "He's fine. Now you have to let him be fine." Sitting in the sun with Max, I realized, like my mother before me, that after a certain point there is nothing more I can do to help, except to love my boys as I love my sister, with a depth of uncon- ditional pleasure I feel in my bones.

We don't forget. In my home, two of my brother's sailboats rest in a windowsill, only occasionally noticed. When I read student drafts in my bedroom, I rest my feet on the footstool Geoff built and then sat on near the warmth of the fireplace as my father read to us at night.

If I want to, I can see Geoff building it in the basement of Tobac- co Road, at his tool bench littered with nails and cans, hammers and screwdrivers, pieces of wire, electrical tape, glue. He saws each piece carefully, chisels grooves into the bottom of the seat, then clamps each piece to sand its edges. He pushes the legs into the gluey grooves, var- nishes each surface, twice. I can feel him silently, patiently measuring, pressing wood to wood, smelling the shellac, his gaze bent attentively over his work. This is proof—he was once here, his hands capable, his desire to create a genuine pleasure.

That is the boy I wish I could share with my sons. And this is the greatest loss—that instead of being able to speak openly and lovingly of that creative, complicated boy, all he became that night long ago was a SUICIDE. The death that cannot be spoken. The stigma that must be hushed. The horror that must be let go. The legacy that must be avoided. But he was a boy. A good boy. And as I write these words he is here again, as he was, full of life, full of art, full of thoughtfulness and feeling.

And so the history rises up to grasp my heart, reminds me again, it can't be dismissed, or ignored, for good. And maybe that's as it should be. Like Flannery O'Connor's sense of Christ, lurking behind the trees, impossible to escape, this history is part of me, no matter how rationally I try to shut it away into categories, explanations, a psychological room of its own. Like O'Connor's sense of grace, it just appears, unasked for but inevitable, and exactly what I unwittingly need sometimes, a reminder of primal truths. Perhaps this is what grief finally becomes, burned deeply into the brain, then burnished through each stage of life–a private set of cues and responses, one's own stations of the Cross, a way of accepting, and honoring, so one can move forward, once again.

ABOUT THE AUTHOR

Beth Taylor is a Senior Lecturer in the English Department's Nonfiction Writing Program at Brown University in Providence, Rhode Island.

LaVergne, TN USA
22 September 2009
158515LV00003BA/1/P